from the library of

....

....

CLASSIC
CRAFTS *and* RECIPES
for the HOLIDAYS

Christmas with Martha Stewart Living

CLASSIC
CRAFTS *and* RECIPES
for the HOLIDAYS

Originally published in book form by Martha Stewart Living
Omnimedia, Inc. in 2001. Published simultaneously by
Clarkson Potter/Publishers, Oxmoor House, Inc., and Leisure Arts.

A portion of this work was previously published in
MARTHA STEWART LIVING.

Printed in the United States of America.

Library of Congress Cataloging-in-Publication Data

Classic crafts and recipes for the holidays/by the editors of
Martha Stewart Living.
Includes index.
1. Christmas decorations. 2. Handicraft. 3. Christmas Cookery.
I. Title: Christmas with Martha Stewart Living. II. Martha
Stewart Living.
TT9000.C4 C53 2001
745.594'12—dc21   20010211275

ISBN 0-8487-2434-8 (hardcover)
    0-8487-2435-6 (paperback)

CONTENTS

the HOLIDAY
SEASON

The most cherished memories of my childhood have to do with the holiday season. The second-eldest child in a family of eight, I looked forward to trimming the tree, baking cookies, making presents, and giving parties. Frugality, although inspired by lack of funds, never left us needy. Mother and Father encouraged us to be inventive, industrious. We'd spend months crafting gifts for one another: a hand-smocked pinafore for the baby, a hand-knit six-foot-long cable scarf for Father (he lost it the first time he wore it), and hand-made dolls' dresses. But one gift we received from our parents outlasted all others: They told us to strive for the best, to follow our hearts. The holidays taught us much about family unity and style and loving and fun. * Father took the family car from Nutley, New Jersey, to his salesman's job each morning, so once a week our next-door neighbors drove my mother and me to the stores for a family shopping trip. (In a week, we'd usually spend thirty-two dollars for

food and homekeeping supplies, including the milk, buttermilk, and cream that were delivered.) For special holiday feasts, we'd buy fresh, fat capons, fresh fish, nuts of every

Choosing the Christmas tree has always been one of our happiest family traditions. Every year, as I search for the fullest, most perfectly shaped evergreen, I am reminded of that enormous blue spruce our family put up so many years ago.

sort, and bundles of local farm produce. * Every season we chose the Christmas tree together. One year we decided to cut down the enormous blue spruce in our front yard, convinced that the top would make the best of all our trees. It was much, much too large, and it dwarfed our living room; the yard always looked barren afterward. But we laughed at our mistake. * We still laugh. We remember. And we follow the traditions established by our grandparents, all the while creating our own golden moments that our children, and their children, will recall with joy in years to come. * *Martha Stewart*

CRANBERRIES

the color of christmas

*

More than any other fruit, the cranberry belongs to Christmas. Its deep scarlet color is tailor-made for holiday decorating, and its flavor—at once fresh, tart, and sweet—is worth celebrating in itself. Cranberries have long been a part of classic holiday rituals, particularly in North America, where they are native and abundant in the fall and winter. It may have been their very abundance that made them a tradition. Unlike more elaborate ornaments or elusive ingredients, the crimson berries could be collected in quantity even when other resources were scarce; they were generously piled into bowls, cooked into luscious sauces, and strung with popcorn into garlands for the tree. Memories of cozy evenings spent with family, sipping hot chocolate and stringing garlands like those, continue to inspire our holiday efforts.

It makes you wonder why, today, cranberries at holiday time are so often reduced to something that comes in a can. That familiar cylinder of jellied cranberry sauce is a far cry from the plump, mouth-puckering berries themselves; their personality is all but lost in the transformation. Still, many people insist on serving canned cranberry sauce on the holiday table. Go ahead and offer it if a picky eater or a sentimental tradition demands. But by no means stop there.

Cranberries lend themselves to all sorts of holiday gifts and craft projects. Baked into crumbly almond cookies, they provide flecks of festive color and just the right sharp, sweet burst of flavor. Vodka or other clear spirits, when infused

CRANBERRY PRESENTS *Sleek glass bottles make charming gifts when filled with cranberry vinegar; sequins on metallic thread look like tiny berries themselves. Pistachio-Cranberry Biscotti (top) and Chewy Cranberry-Almond Cookies (bottom), tucked inside gift boxes, travel well.*

with cranberry, can be decanted into glass bottles to make excellent hostess gifts. The cranberry is a culinary chameleon, as suitable for a creamy sorbet as for a savory cornbread stuffing. And of course there's the sauce: When the berries are cooked just until bursting, their flavor mellowed and balanced by a sweet twist of citrus, the result is incomparable. The most dramatic role played by cranberries, however, is as decoration: They can drip like strands of rubies from the mantel, fill gleaming compotes, or substitute for flower frogs to support stems in curvy glass vases.

However you choose to incorporate cranberries into your holidays, you'll be doing so in a tradition that is centuries old. The berries grow wild in sandy, lowland bogs across much of North America, particularly in the Cape Cod region of Massachusetts, as well as in New Jersey, Wisconsin, and Washington. They were a wintertime staple in Native American diets and were included in the earliest settlers' holiday feasts. They quickly became a favorite accompaniment for meat at Colonial meals and provided a principal source of vitamin C for sailors traveling from the Americas. The name, according to some historians, came from the blossom that hangs down from a slender stem, said to resemble the head of a crane. Thus, they came to be known as *crane berries*. Others argue that the name came from the birds that frequented the bogs to gobble up the berries. Whichever is correct, the term was eventually shortened to the modern word *cranberry*.

Despite their importance as a food source, the crops were not actively cultivated until the early nineteenth century. Today, commercial cranberry bogs thrive, and each fall, thousands of acres of land are covered with crimson blankets of ripe fruit. Cranberries are harvested, either wet, by large harvesting machines that beat the berries from their vines so they will float in a flooded bog for easy collecting, or dry—picked by machine and carefully gathered in burlap bags, then airlifted from the bogs in crates, since these areas are unreachable by truck. The dry-harvested berries are always the best of the crop—firm and fresh, plump and light enough to bounce into the air like tiny rubber balls. Wet-harvested berries are reserved for juice and other processed foods. It is the dry berries that are sold fresh and fresh-frozen in your local grocery store and that form the basis of the recipes and projects on the following pages.

Most fresh cranberry decorations will last about a month outdoors or in a cool spot; when exposed to heat, they will likely get soft and spoil sooner. Whatever you do, enjoy them while they last. In the market, look for firm, brightly colored, plump fruits with no signs of shriveling. These will have the best flavor and last the longest on display. Remember that any decoration using fresh produce will have a limited life span, so plan accordingly when preparing for a party or other event. If you run short on time, don't worry about getting too elaborate—the greatest beauty of these berries is their jewel-like simplicity.

HOLIDAY SIDEBOARD *A rich-brown turkey finished with a cranberry glaze is the centerpiece of a spectacular Christmas sideboard. The bird is generously stuffed with Cranberry-Cornbread Stuffing. Side dishes include buttery Green Pea Purée and two cranberry sauces: a cognac-laced condiment and a chilled relish of cranberries, oranges, hot pepper, and celery. Tiny garlands of fresh cranberries are taped to pedestal cake stands holding candles. A box-wood wreath is wrapped in a single strand of cranberries.* OPPOSITE: *A burlap sack holds freshly picked, dry-harvest cranberries. These are the berries most prized for holiday sauces and other cooking, as well as for decorating.*

HOLIDAY SPIRITS *Presents of vodka infused with cranberry and blood orange are wrapped to sparkle with sequins.*

FLAVORED VODKA

YOU WILL NEED *fresh fruit, including cranberries, blood oranges, and pineapple • wide-mouth glass jars • vodka • decorative bottles*

Add sliced fruit or whole cranberries to a clean glass jar. Decant vodka into the jar, cover it tightly, and refrigerate for one to two weeks. Transfer the infused vodka into a decorative bottle; you can store it for up to six months (keep it in the refrigerator if you leave the fruit in the bottle). If using pineapple, strain the fruit out completely before storing. See The Recipes.

CRANBERRY SORBET *Some sorbets are ethereal, icy concoctions intended as palate cleansers between courses. This is not one of those. Made with fresh cranberries and naturally low-fat buttermilk, this fruit-flecked sorbet is creamy and rich tasting; served with cookies, it will hold its own on the dessert table—especially if the dessert dishes are clear glass.*

MANTELSCAPE *There is a fiery drama to a holiday mantel wearing nothing but red: Abundant bouquets of roses, tulips, and carnations crown cranberry-filled vases. The berries stand in for flower frogs—be sure to use fresh, firm ones, discarding any that are soft or have burst. Glass compotes are heaped with more berries. For garlands, loosely string fresh cranberries onto heavy-duty thread. Hang them from eye hooks (available from hardware stores) screwed into the underside of the mantel and the back of the mirror. Form two long strands for the draping garlands, then smaller pieces for the drops, looping and hanging them from each hook.*

CRANBERRY UPSIDE-DOWN CAKE *The classic American upside-down cake is typically made with pineapple rings. In this version, a layer of cranberries, simmered in maple syrup and cinnamon just until soft, makes a gorgeous topping once the cake is turned out of its pan. Placed on a pedestal, it can serve as the centerpiece for a Christmas dessert buffet; it is equally appealing with a quiet cup of tea during a break from the holiday rush. Offer biscotti as well for nibblers.*

SEE THE RECIPES

TURKEYS

I have KNOWN

Eating deep-fried turkey at Joel Silver's plantation in South Carolina made me think about all the different turkeys I have enjoyed over the years. Although most of them were roasted in an oven—only Joel's was immersed in boiling-hot peanut oil—there were subtle and sometimes not-so-subtle differences that made each a unique experience. ✳ My mother's turkey is the one I know best. She had a smallish wall oven that limited the size of her bird—twenty-eight pounds was about all it could manage. Her stuffing was always made from two-day-old sliced white bread, chestnuts (roasted by Dad the night before), sausage meat, lots of chopped celery, apples, onions, fresh parsley, dried sage, raw eggs, salt, pepper, and Bell's Seasoning. Mother used an old enameled roasting pan, but never aluminum foil, preferring that the drippings collect in the pan for the gravy. Water, stock, and melted butter were used for basting the bird. Mother roasted it at 350 degrees for about fifteen minutes a pound, a method that took from six to seven hours. That's why the turkey went in at 7:00 A.M. ✳ A number of years ago, I raised seven magnificent broad-breasted bronze turkeys and gave them to my best friends. Memrie Lewis was the recipient of the biggest—a forty-pound tom. When her housekeeper, Mimi, saw the bird, her eyes grew large, and she laughed nervously. Memrie's oven was as small as my mother's. With great consternation, the stuffing (a delectable buttery cornbread mixture) was inserted, the oven heated, and the turkey plopped into the pan, badly overhanging all four sides. A bit of surgery (wing tips and tail) and a homemade heavy-foil oven liner allowed them to push the bird into the oven and force the door closed. That turkey was so fresh and young it roasted at 375 degrees for less than five hours and was done to perfection, albeit minus the parson's nose, its absence nicely camouflaged with fresh herbs. ✳ That year I also attended a midday meal at my sister Kathy's home in Old Greenwich, Connecticut. Kathy roasts her turkey in a convection oven to speed the process for a juicier bird. She starts the turkey at 400 degrees and gradually turns down the oven to 325, testing the bird with a meat thermometer until done (180 degrees). Her turkey, too, was absolutely wonderful. ✳ My friend Jane Heller has an interesting repertoire of rather complicated recipes. In one, the more than fifty ingredients and the precise way in which they must be applied to the surface of the turkey—every fifteen minutes for hours on end—appeal to Jane, who has been roasting "her bird" accordingly for many years. ✳ One year I got it into my head to cover my turkey with a decorative crust of pâté feuilletée (puff pastry), a recipe much like beef Wellington. I had to improvise, prebaking a fifteen-pound hen, cooling it, covering it with a sheet of puff pastry, applying puff-pastry leaves and shapes, and glazing the whole thing with cream and egg yolk. Baked right before serving, it was indeed a spectacular presentation. I missed the crispy skin of my regular roasting method, but for pomp and show, nothing will ever beat it. ✳ My English friend Julia Booth-Clibborn enjoys a big bird once or twice a year. Sometimes she cooks hers partially boned, stuffed with forcemeat, the turkey encasing a boned stuffed pheasant, which encases a third boned fowl, perhaps a partridge or grouse. Cut crosswise, like a French galantine, hers is by far the most elaborate and unusual of any bird I have ever tasted. ✳ However you prepare your turkey, I hope you will let it remind

For my most unusual turkey yet, I enlisted master pastry chef and chocolatier Rémy Fünfrock to create for a magazine cover, an eighteen-inch, solid-chocolate turkey, in an antique mold given to me by Sharon Patrick, MSLO President and C.O.O.

you, as each of mine reminds me, to be thankful—for the abundance of the holidays, and for the people who share them with you. ✳ *Martha Stewart*

ICE

crystalline decorations

There's a quiet wonder to the world after a winter storm. The snow stops falling, and sunlight illuminates tree branches and berry-studded shrubs encased in glistening ice. For a time, the spectacular artwork of nature takes center stage. Such miracles happen by chance, but you can imitate nature's process; all you need are a few freezing days and some simple ingredients to create your own icy holiday decorations.

Wreaths, tree ornaments, even candle votives made of ice are easy to assemble, and you needn't go much farther than your own backyard for the necessary materials. Send the kids out to gather sprigs of evergreen; ask a neighbor to share some colorful berries if your own property is lacking. Wash your hands after handling inedible berries.

If you plan to make the ice decorations for food presentation—as with our hors d'oeuvres tray on page 26—use edible items, such as fresh herbs and cranberries. Keep decorations chilled in ordinary containers—the freezer, an ice chest, or outdoors if it's cold enough. For ice clarity, distilled water works best, but be aware that air bubbles will still cloud the ice, no matter what. When you remove the projects from their molds, expect some crackling; this just adds to their charm.

Display your ice creations in prominent places, where the freezing winter air will keep them intact for as long as possible. Of course, any decoration made of ice will eventually melt away; like the holiday season itself, its fleeting beauty is part of what makes it so memorable.

ICE WREATH *Winter's are the shortest, darkest days of the year, but they are illuminated by the brilliance of snow and ice. A savarin tin shaped this winterberry wreath. The decorations on the following pages, all made of natural materials frozen in ice, were inspired by the icebound landscape.*

WREATHS AND STARS

YOU WILL NEED *greenery and berries • savarin and cookie molds • ribbon • twine*

The best way to ensure that patterns hold their shapes is to freeze them twice, in layers. For wreaths, such as the mini-eucalyptus and pink-pepperberry one below, place greenery and berries in savarin mold (see The Guide), allowing branches and leaves to protrude; fill with a little water, and freeze. Fill, and freeze again. Carefully unmold, using lukewarm water to dislodge. Hang by slipping a wide ribbon under top of wreath, and tie ends in a bow. For stars, attach twine to a spray or twig, tape to inside top of mold, and freeze using two-step process above.

WHAT FREEZES WELL *Flora that holds up under ice includes (opposite): most evergreens, such as hemlock (1), yew (9), and juniper (11); many fresh and dried berries, including winterberries or Christmas berries (4), which grow in much of the United States; pink pepperberries (8)—look for these in dried form at your florist's shop; most common holly (10); and golden-red American bittersweet (6), a northeastern native. Any variety of long-lasting eucalyptus (5, 7), available at your local florist, will also freeze well, as will hardy privet (3). When using berries, completely submerge them in ice; otherwise, oxidation will cause their color to fade and bleed into surrounding areas. Cranberries (2) must be very fresh (not frozen) before you freeze them.*

Nº. 2
cranberry

Nº. 1
hemlock

Nº. 3
privet

Nº. 4
winterberry

Nº. 7
seeded eucalyptus

Nº. 5
mini eucalyptus

Nº. 6
American bittersweet

Nº. 8
pink pepperberry

Nº. 9
yew

Nº. 10
holly

Nº. 11
juniper

TREE TRIMMING *Adorn an outdoor Christmas tree with festive jingle balls, wreaths, and stars. These small ice ornaments should last for two or three days; even when the temperature is below freezing, the sun and wind will eventually wear them away.*

ICE ORNAMENTS

YOU WILL NEED *greenery and berries ·
two-part spherical-cube trays · twine ·
tweezers · savarin and cookie molds*

For jingle balls, place greenery and berries in bottom of spherical-cube tray. To make hangers for balls, place twine across the top of each pair of molds, bring ends around, and tie loosely on underside. Add water to fill. Fit top tray onto bottom. Fill spheres with water; freeze. To unmold, dip tray in lukewarm water. Snip twine connecting pairs of balls. For wreaths or stars, use tweezers to set greenery and berries in molds. Once frozen, tie with twine hangers. For stars, attach twine to a spray or twig, tape to inside top of mold, and freeze using two-step process (see "wreaths and stars" on page 22).

NOEL BLOCKS

YOU WILL NEED *greenery and berries · rectangular baking pans · twine*

This Christmas greeting was fashioned out of mini eucalyptus and winterberries, frozen in ordinary baking pans. You can also use other greenery with close-lying leaves or needles, such as hemlock or short-needle evergreen. Arrange the ice blocks on the lawn or an outdoor wall (wooden porches and windowsills may suffer water damage as the temperature rises). For each letter, place mini-eucalyptus sprays in baking pan (above); to secure the shapes, wrap twine around the ends where the sprays meet. Arrange berries. Cover with a quarter inch of water; freeze to secure the pattern. Add enough water to fill; freeze again. To unmold, let blocks melt briefly at room temperature, or dip briefly in a tub of warm water.

ICED VODKA

YOU WILL NEED *30-gauge floral wire * greenery and berries * bottle of vodka * monofilament * half-gallon milk carton*

To make the eucalyptus bottle, use floral wire to form greenery and berries into three small wreaths. Place two wreaths around base and shoulder of a clean, label-free bottle of vodka; attach third to center of bottle with clear monofilament—tie line to each side of wreath, wrap around bottle, and tie in back. Place bottle in milk carton. Fill carton with water, leaving about an inch of bottle neck showing. Freeze undisturbed for at least twenty-four hours. For the winterberry bottle, place bottle in carton, scatter berries around base, fill with two inches of water, and freeze. Then add water up to bottle's shoulder, place berry wreath in center, and freeze again. Add another ring of loose berries, fill with water, and freeze a third time. To serve, rip carton from ice; smooth ice with cloth dipped in warm water.

HORS D'OEUVRES ON ICE

YOU WILL NEED *large rectangular baking pan * duct tape * fresh herbs and berries * serving tray*

A decorated block of ice is an elegant serving tray for chilled buffet food, such as boiled shrimp (see The Recipes). To make tray (left), fill a large baking pan (if not watertight, secure edges with duct tape) almost to the top with water, and freeze undisturbed for at least twenty-four hours. Then dampen the top of the ice block, and arrange fresh herbs and cranberries or other edible berries around the edges to create a border. Freeze for a short time to secure pattern, then fill with more water, allowing some greenery to poke through, and freeze again. Carefully remove block from pan by submerging bottom in warm water. This step can be awkward, since the pan is large and heavy; you may need someone to help. Place block on a larger serving tray, and arrange hors d'oeuvres.

FROSTY COCKTAILS *Frozen vodka bottles, adorned with wreaths of mini eucalyptus, red winterberries, and dried pink pepperberries, make a festive offering on a holiday party bar. Set bottles on a waterproof tray to protect the table, and have a towel on hand for pouring.*

BUCKET AND CUP VOTIVES

YOU WILL NEED *buckets and plastic cups in various sizes ∗ greenery and berries ∗ skewer ∗ stones ∗ candles*

A collection of ice votives lining a stone wall will warmly welcome guests to a winter gathering. The flickering candlelight silhouettes the greenery and berries encased in the ice. **1.** To create a large votive, center a smaller bucket inside a larger one; tape top edges together so that they are level. Insert greenery, using a skewer to arrange in desired pattern. Carefully pour a little water into space between buckets, and weigh down smaller bucket with a few stones. Freeze until solid. Repeat two or three times, adding greenery and water, until form is complete. To unmold, remove inner bucket by filling center with warm water; immerse outer bucket in sink or larger vessel of warm water. Place candle in center, and light. **2.** For cup votives, repeat process for bucket votives using plastic cups of varied sizes. Unmold with lukewarm water.

NUTS

sweet and savory

*

Nuts are ubiquitous during the holidays, but subtly so. We chop them for cakes and cookies, or mix them with bread and herbs and stuff them in turkeys; we fill bowls with them and place them strategically around the house to be cracked open and gobbled up between meals. Even their aroma plays a part in the holiday drama: Wafting from a bag of freshly roasted chestnuts, for example, the scent works in concert with seasonal music and frosty windows to create an atmosphere that inspires sentimental reveries. Nuts, in all their forms, are plentiful at this time of year and always manage to work their way into yuletide celebrations. And yet rarely do they take center stage.

Given the chance, however, nuts can improve upon almost any holiday tradition—ornamental or culinary. Their shells are strong and naturally decorative, making them ideal for keepsakes and craft projects. And the contents of those shells, the sweet, crunchy kernels hiding inside, are flavorful enough to form the basis of any number of rich holiday dishes. They are an indulgence, of course: Most nuts (the chestnut is one notable exception) are high in fat and calories. But at the holidays, a little indulgence is exactly what you want. So why not make the most of them?

Fresh from their shells, nuts taste of the woods, the way real maple syrup and birch beer do. Some, like the popular southern pecan, are dense, chewy, and sweet; others, such as the tropical macadamia, are so crisp and buttery they will almost melt in your mouth. Most nuts are harvested in the fall

FAVOR TREE *Nutshell ornaments and nut-filled paper cones and boxes dangle from a tabletop tree. Host a trimming party for your usual tree, then invite guests to dismantle this smaller one; beaded garlands, nutshell ornaments, and glass balls will remain when all the favors are claimed.*

and develop their best flavor by the holiday season. When shopping, look for nuts that are heavy for their size, smooth-skinned, and free of blemishes. If you are buying them in the shell, shake a few in the grocer's display; if they rattle, put them back—that is a sign that the nut meats within are dried and shriveled. Shelled or unshelled, nuts aren't as durable as they appear. Heat, moisture, and air can make their natural oils go rancid. Be sure to store any shelled nuts that you won't use right away in the refrigerator—or better, the freezer—in airtight plastic bags or containers. There the hardiest will last for up to a year; the most delicate will spoil much sooner. Their scent will give them away; rancid nuts have a noticeable off-odor.

If you happen to be lucky enough to have any kind of nut tree in your yard, you will likely have a plentiful supply every autumn for years to come. Most nut trees are famously long-lived: There are walnut groves in Italy and France, for example, that include trees more than three hundred years old. The pecan trees that George Washington planted at Mount Vernon still bear nuts each fall. And harvesting them couldn't be any easier—most nuts fall from their branches when they are ripe; to harvest them you need only pick them up off the ground.

The nuts you gather outdoors should be stored in much the same way as those you buy from the market, but you have to prepare them first: Remove the husks around the shells, if there are any, as soon as possible, and burn them, since the husks can harbor pests. Submerge the nuts in their shells in a bucket of water; the good ones will sink.

Discard any that float, and hang the rest in a wire basket to dry. Store unshelled nuts in a cool, dry place, such as a basement or a garage. Crack only as many as you're ready to eat at one time; the rest will keep better if they are left in their shells. Once the warm weather of summer arrives, of course, you'll need to take steps to keep them fresh: At that point, crack the remaining nuts and store the kernels in the freezer or refrigerator, in a sealed plastic bag or airtight container.

For most of the craft projects on the following pages, you can substitute your favorite nuts for the ones that we have used. Any of the ones included in a typical selection found in a grocery store—such as walnuts, almonds, hazelnuts, Brazil nuts, and pecans—can be gilded and strung for ornaments or glued onto forms to make wreaths and topiaries. If you can find them, you might also want to include a few more exotic types, such as heartnuts or section nuts; these have distinctive shells with an appealing decorative effect. If you would like to use nuts to make lockets and little keepsake boxes, walnuts are your best choice, since the design of their shells makes them easy to split open into perfect halves.

After the projects and celebrating are done, the remaining nuts from the season's supply will be at their best when presented simply—taken out of their shells and tucked into pretty gift boxes. For centuries, such gifts have been offered at weddings, holidays, and other celebrations as symbols of abundance and good fortune. There could be no more fitting message for the holiday season.

NUT GLOSSARY *Though tasty, beechnuts (1) are tiny and rarely eaten—except by wild birds. The hican (2) is a savory cross between the hickory and pecan. Though not grown commercially, the shagbark hickory (3) and shellbark hickory (10) thrive east of the Mississippi. The heartnut (4) is a Japanese walnut variety with no bitter aftertaste. The buartnut (5) is a cross between the butternut and the heartnut. Pistachios (6) are prized for their green meats and sweet fragrance. The hazelnut (7, 12) is known as the filbert in Oregon, where most of America's crop is grown. More like a grain than a nut, the chestnut (8) has only two percent fat and seventy calories an ounce. Pine nuts (9), or pignoli, are delicate and last just a month in the refrigerator. The crimson-skinned red walnut (11) looks striking but tastes like other walnuts. The pecan (13), from the American South, has a rich, warm taste. The hearty-flavored English walnut (14) actually originated in the Middle East, so botanists call it the Persian walnut. The elegant, Asian-born almond (15) grows in abundance in California. The tropical macadamia (16) has a mellow, buttery taste and is seventy-three percent fat.*

Nº 1
*jenner
beechnut*

Nº 2
*bixby
hican*

Nº 3
*campbell shagbark
hickory*

Nº 4
*fodermaier
heartnut*

Nº 5
*mitchell
buartnut*

Nº 6
*kerman
pistachio*

Nº 7
*fitzgerald
hazelnut*

Nº 8
*colossal
chestnut*

Nº 9
*Korean
pine nut*

Nº 10
*fayette shellbark
hickory*

Nº 11
red walnut

Nº 12
*gallaty 502
hazelnut*

Nº 13
*snaps
pecan*

Nº 14
*Persian
(English)
walnut*

Nº 15
fritz almond

Nº 16
*cate
macadamia*

ORNAMENT TREATS *The French traditionally present new babies with paper cones filled with blue or pink almond candies. Our variations on this theme, below, are cones, boxes, and cups loaded with nuts for great seasonal favors. The delicate ornaments are nutshells gilded with mica powders (opposite page).*

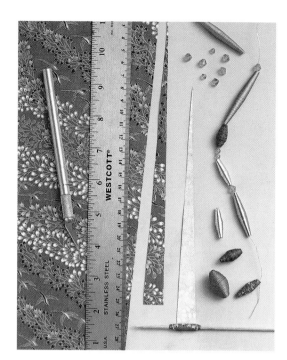

PAPER BEAD GARLAND

YOU WILL NEED *light- to medium-weight paper ∗ utility knife ∗ eighth-inch wooden skewer ∗ heavy-duty thread or fishing line ∗ glass or plastic beads*

Any foil, craft paper, or wallpaper can become a string of beads (see tree, page 30) with a little creative rolling. Using a ruler, mark off points along one side of the paper at intervals equal to the desired width of the beads. On opposite side of paper, mark off points at set intervals, but make first point one half-width in from edge of paper. Line up ruler diagonally from point to point, and cut out long, triangular strips with a utility knife. Wrap the wide end of a strip around an eighth-inch wooden skewer, rolling tightly for two turns. Apply a very thin strip of glue vertically along the middle of the paper, and continue rolling into a bead shape—keeping edges symmetrical. Slide the skewer out of the bead, and let dry. String onto heavy-duty thread or fishing line, alternating with smaller glass or plastic beads, if desired.

NUT CUPS AND CONES

YOU WILL NEED *photocopier ∗ medium-weight paper ∗ PMA adhesive ∗ vellum ∗ bone folder ∗ brush and craft glue ∗ trim ∗ nuts ∗ cord or ribbon*

Because nuts tend to be oily, paper containers should be lined with vellum or waxed paper. **1.** Photocopy templates on page 133, and trace shapes onto paper. Line the paper: Press sheet of PMA adhesive onto one side to make a sticky surface; press vellum on top. Cut out shape. With bone folder, score paper on fold lines; fold into shape. **2.** Close along one side with craft glue. Decorate each cone with trim or lacy motifs from paper doilies. Fill with nuts; make two holes in each wide flap of lid, and close with fancy cord or ribbon, which can double as a hanger for the tree.

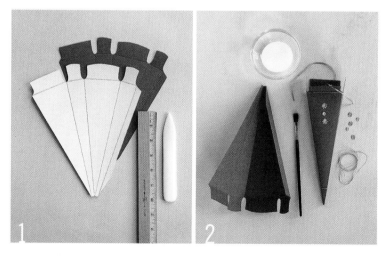

GILDING NUTS

YOU WILL NEED *paintbrushes · nuts · water-based sizing · mica powders*

Because nuts have naturally decorative shapes, they become jewel-like when embellished with lustrous colors. They can be hung as ornaments, attached to ribbons to dress up a dining table, or strung as a garland. For our projects, we used hazelnuts, walnuts, pecans, and section nuts—which split naturally on one end into three even sections. You can use any whole nuts with shapes that you like. **1.** Use a small paintbrush to cover the entire surface of each nut with sizing, and allow to dry until the sizing is tacky, about fifteen minutes (follow label instructions). **2.** Use a larger brush to apply mica powders to the surface; brush away the excess, and then set it aside to let it dry completely. Mica powders, available in stores that sell faux-finishing products, are easy to work with and, unlike more traditional bronzing materials, are non-toxic. However, it is still wise to wear a dust mask when working with these or any other fine-powdered products.

NUT ORNAMENTS

YOU WILL NEED *gold or silver twine · gilded nuts · hot-glue gun · glass or plastic beads*

Gilded nutshells need little more than their sparkle to impart holiday glamour. You can turn them into ornaments by attaching simple hangers: Wrap a length of thin gold or silver twine around the nut, and hot-glue in place. Then carefully attach glass or plastic beads to the nutshell; be sure to glue one bead to the top center, leaving the holes unobstructed on both sides. Thread twine through that bead, and tie a loop for hanging.

NUT NAPKIN RINGS *Gilded nuts attached to short lengths of satin ribbon make one-of-a-kind napkin rings: Hot-glue ribbons into rings, folding over top edges for smooth seams. (Length depends on girth of rolled napkin.) For section nut and hazelnut (far left, center left), attach a bead to the top of a nut, loop heavy-duty thread through the bead, and tack to the ribbon. A gilded walnut-shell half (center right) is hot-glued flat against the ribbon. The larger section nut (far right) is threaded with thin gold cording, which is tied to a second ribbon.*

WALNUT GIFT BOXES

YOU WILL NEED *walnuts • awl • water-based sizing • paintbrushes • mica powders • stiff brush • metallic trim • narrow velvet ribbon*

1. Pry shells apart with awl, pushing away from hand for safety. Empty the shells that break evenly, and coat inside with sizing. Let dry until tacky; brush with mica powders. Let dry. Use stiff brush to burnish to a shine. **2.** With a tiny bit of glue, attach trim around edges of nut halves; hold in place until dry. Join nut halves by gluing a length of narrow velvet ribbon across seam to make a hinge; continue gluing ribbon up both halves of shell, forming a loop at the top on one side. Slide other side through the loop to close box and to serve as a hanger.

LOCKET ORNAMENTS

YOU WILL NEED *awl • walnuts • parchment paper • photographs • color photocopier • craft glue • utility knife • metallic trim • ½-inch velvet ribbon • hot-glue gun • plastic beads • metallic thread*

Using an awl, split the walnuts, and empty their contents, as in walnut gift boxes, above. Place nut, open side down, on parchment, trace around outline of nut, and cut out shape. Enlarge photos on a color photocopier to desired size (there's no need to cut original photos), and place parchment template around the desired part of the photocopied image. Trace around template with pencil, then cut out image. With a small amount of craft glue, attach the image to the walnut half, pressing as glue sets. Turn nut, flat side down, and trim away any excess paper with a utility knife. Glue metallic trim around nut halves to make a frame. Glue velvet ribbon across seam to make a hinge. On the opposite side, hot-glue two plastic beads in place to form a clasp, and close with metallic thread. If you use a single photo, glue a decorative paper in the other half to complete the locket.

GIFT PACKAGING *Some walnuts crack haphazardly, but others grow with perfect seams and break into smooth, even halves with gentle coaxing. This natural construction makes them ideal as gift boxes for tiny treasures. Colorfully gild the inside, loop each walnut with a narrow velvet ribbon that will serve as both hinge and clasp, and hang the packages like ornaments from the branches of a tree.*

NUT WREATH

YOU WILL NEED *twelve-inch straw wreath form * unshelled mixed nuts * hot-glue gun * satin ribbon*

The contrasting textures and deep, earthy colors of nuts in their shells make a warm alternative to the traditional ring of yule-tide greenery. To construct this wreath, it is important to use a wreath form of adequate size; the nuts will be overcrowded in the center of a form that's too small. Hot-glue the nuts one at a time to three sides of the form, puzzling them together so that the shapes work together. Leave the back flat so the wreath will hang nicely. Finish with a wide, chocolate-brown satin bow.

NUT TOPIARY

YOU WILL NEED *unshelled mixed nuts * hot-glue gun * Styrofoam cone and ball * miniature green and gold glass balls * urn * Popsicle stick*

Choose a selection of whole mixed nuts, as are used to make the nut wreath, above. Hot-glue the nuts to the cone-shaped form one at a time, arranging them as you work to create a desirable pattern. Glue miniature green and gold glass Christmas balls between the nuts for added interest. When the cone is completely covered, cut Styrofoam ball in half, and fit one half into the urn, with the rounded side down. Push a Popsicle stick part of the way into the bottom of the cone form, and press the other end into the half-ball in the urn; this will create a steady base to hold the cone upright. Nut topiaries and wreaths require patience to construct. If stored correctly, however, they will last for years; keep in a cool spot, wrapped in plastic, with plenty of mothballs to ward off pests.

TIMELESS ARRANGEMENTS *Mixed-nut topiaries give sculptural presence to a holiday mantel. For the garland, nut ornaments (page 35) were strung on gold twine and wired into greenery. Clusters of nut ornaments were also hot-glued to the wire holding the greenery together.*

SAVORY HOLIDAY FARE CLOCKWISE, FROM TOP LEFT: *Wide pasta is tossed with a rich sauce of white wine, cream, thyme, and three kinds of nuts—chestnuts, hazelnuts, and pine nuts; the warm pasta absorbs most of the liquid from the sauce. Roasted Cornish game hens rest on a dressing of brown and wild rice and pecans; the little birds are stuffed with some of the mixture, and the rest is baked separately before the serving platter is arranged. Baked Almond Brioche Toasts befit a special breakfast; thick slices of the eggy bread are spread with sweet almond cream and sliced almonds, then toasted.*

SWEET AND SALTY TREATS CLOCKWISE, FROM BELOW: *Gifts of Hazelnut Brittle are wrapped in parchment paper and sealed with drops of amber caramel. For cocktail-party nibbles, sweet raw pecans, walnuts, almonds, and cashews are tossed with spices and baked until crunchy and golden. Whole unsalted nuts crowd the top of this extravagant Chocolate Macadamia-Nut Tart. A garland of acorns, made following the nut-ornaments technique on page 35 and strung with beads on thin gold twine, is tacked at intervals around the tablecloth.*

COOKIE BOXES *Lightweight vellum gift boxes hold a selection of nut cookies. To make the boxes, use the template on page 134, and trace the shapes onto vellum, art paper, or card stock. Fold along lines, and close along one side with double-sided tape. Then secure a band of decorative paper onto the bottom with double-sided tape. Tie the boxes closed with twine, and attach a nut ornament.*

PISTACHIO CHARLOTTE *If there's ever a time for dressy desserts, it's at Christmas, when the whole house wears holiday finery. This glamorous charlotte has rich layers of Pistachio Bavarian Cream and Praline, daintily clasped by ladyfingers. Ready-made ladyfingers will do, but we offer a recipe in case you want every last detail to be homemade.*

SEE THE RECIPES

VISIONS *of*
SUGARPLUMS

When I was a child I was given a cookbook filled with recipes appropriate for a youngster of eight. That at least was what the book said, although it included instructions for flipping crêpes in hot skillets, beating batters with electric hand mixers, and heating sugar to the hard-ball stage (250 degrees) to make candies. My mother obviously was not too concerned with my dexterity since she gave me, from a very early age, complete freedom in her kitchen. It was nice to be trusted, and it encouraged me to experiment and create freely. ✳ I loved that first cookbook. It was large, it had funny sketch-like drawings, and every recipe in it worked. Although the recipes were pretty simple, they didn't take shortcuts or substitute artificial ingredients for good ones. My favorite recipe was for hard butterscotch candy, made from caramelized sugar, cornstarch, cream, and butter. To me, the result was better than any store-bought butterscotch, even the famous foil-wrapped rectangles of Callard & Bowser candy that we could buy at local candy stores. ✳ For holidays, after we made all of our cookies, fruitcakes, and puddings, we would make a selection of unusual confections and candies. We all enjoyed candy making because it was a special treat and because the results so delighted everyone who tasted them. My mother's penuche, which was similar to southern pralines but cut in squares instead of formed into patties, was highly prized. She used freshly shelled South Carolina pecans sent by Uncle Hank. Aunt Clem always made peanut brittle, which was salty as well as sweet because she favored salty Georgia peanuts. I made dozens of caramels and butterscotches, which I wrapped in waxed paper and packed into metal cookie tins that I had handpainted with garden flowers. ✳ We didn't consume much chocolate—I think in those days chocolate was very costly, and imported chocolate wasn't readily available. There was, of course, the popular Hershey brand in the grocery store, and we melted it in a double boiler for fudge and frostings and puddings. At Christmas we all craved chocolate coins wrapped in foil, which were provided by an old-fashioned ice-cream parlor and candy shop called Morris's. At holiday time, this lovely store hand-dipped all of its candies. We children were in the habit of going there to gaze through the window into the candy-making kitchen to watch the complex processes being performed inside. I became very interested in this art and asked a lot of questions and got good answers about chocolate, candy making, and technical stuff like tempering and metal molds. The Morris family was always busy making fantasies that everyone could enjoy. ✳ Candy

making continued to fascinate me as I grew older and traveled to different cities in the United States and around the world. On visits to Atlantic City I observed ladies in pink-and-white-striped dresses kneading and pulling real saltwater taffy on the boardwalk. In Louisiana I tasted real pralines made from local sugar and farm-fresh cream and nuts, and

Marzipan—a ground-almond paste—is like artist's clay; watching master sculptors work with it leaves me in awe. This gift box contains a Washington apple, a Bosc pear, a blood orange, and a Comice pear, adorned with leaves and clove stems.

vowed to perfect my attempts at making these tender candies. In Sicily, in the dark and foreboding city of Catania, I saw to my amazement the intricate and delicious marzipan creations of the master sculptors of the ground almond. And in Paris, on frequent forays to Fauchon, I tasted the sugarplums that are so honored in Tchaikovsky's *The Nutcracker*. ✳ I'll continue to make confections—I hope someday to learn the art of blown sugar so I can make pears and apples and other fruits and objects that resemble Venetian glass. I also dream about making striped and dotted and pulled candy that can be snipped and cut into odd shapes. These techniques will take working with masters, but that for me is what learning is all about. ✳ *Martha Stewart*

CHAPTER 4

AMARYLLIS

the holiday flower

It is perhaps the greatest show of the holiday season: Amaryllis bulbs emerge from a quiet fall of dormancy to sprout enormous, brilliant blooms in true reds, vivid pinks, and whites as luminous as sunlit snow. Many arrive just in time for Christmas. Others come a bit earlier or later, but all last for weeks, providing vibrant color during the holidays and well beyond.

Compared with many other houseplants, the amaryllis is remarkably low-maintenance—it thrives on benign neglect for much of the year—yet it is intensely satisfying in its rewards. The bulbs are inexpensive enough to have many: You can cluster several in the same cozy planter; arrange groupings of pots on the dining table in lieu of a solitary centerpiece; or tuck single bulbs into terra-cotta pots, along with care instructions, for inexpensive, assembly-line holiday gifts. And there is a wide enough choice of colors, styles, and sizes that no two plants need look alike.

In recent years, an increasing number of new varieties of amaryllis have emerged. There are now miniature-flowered types on the market, for example, as well as more double-flowered ones (with frilly-looking blooms that have more than one row of petals) than ever before. Even the range of colors and color patterns is expanding—the picotees, with their delicate bands of darker color on the edges of the petals, are becoming more popular, as are less traditional colors, such as salmon. Every fall, bulb catalogs boast new varieties, luring collectors with novel shapes and hues.

FLOWER SHOW *A vintage wirework plant stand holds a small garden of amaryllis—red and white, single and double, miniature and standard, each in full bloom for the holidays. Annual ryegrass seeds scattered on the soil of each pot create tiny meadows beneath the flowers.*

The biggest surprise about these plants is that they aren't members of the genus *Amaryllis* at all. The big, fat bulbs are in the related genus *Hippeastrum* and descended from plants native to tropical America. The genus *Amaryllis* contains only one species, *A. belladonna;* it comes from South Africa, is still quite rare, and is tricky to grow.

Taxonomy aside, the bulbs we call amaryllis are easy to grow indoors or in a greenhouse. They do not need much room; in fact, they like snug surroundings. A pot about two inches larger in diameter than the bulb is ideal (for example, a six-inch pot for a four-inch-diameter bulb).

A good soil medium will be fast-draining and have plenty of sand, offering a weighty, stiff support. Try a blend of well-rotted compost, coarse sand, and vermiculite in a ratio of 3:3:2.

Do not bury your bulb deeper than its shoulders (be sure to plant pointed side up); at least one-third of it should be above the soil line. Fill the pot partway so the bulb will rest at the correct depth, then fill—tamping the soil with a piece of bamboo cane or a pencil. Water until the soil is moist, then place in a warm, bright spot. Do not water again until signs of green growth appear or three weeks have passed, whichever comes first. The bulb will usually make flowers first—as many as three successive stemfuls in the largest, finest grade—and eventually sprout foliage. When the flowers fade, cut stems to the base, but encourage leaves all spring and summer with bright light, regular watering, and biweekly feeding.

To force a bulb to bloom the next winter, first create a dormant period starting in September by simulating the end of the rainy season: Completely withhold all water and light for about six or eight weeks. (One easy method is to set the pots in a closet.) Then cut off the old foliage, add more soil if necessary, and water thoroughly, beginning anew the steps to allow flowering.

How long an amaryllis takes to flower depends on the bulb. Dutch hybrid varieties can take up to three months. The Christmas-flowering types bloom in about six weeks and sometimes less; these varieties are grown commercially in the warm climate of South Africa, where the seasons are opposite to those of the Northern Hemisphere, so they arrive at flower markets eager to blossom. Such plants typically bear flowers on stiff, shorter stems—about twelve to eighteen inches versus the eighteen to twenty-four-plus inches seen in the Dutch varieties. The longer stems provide a somewhat more graceful display, but for an almost guaranteed Christmas bloom, the African-grown bulbs are your best choice.

For the most beautiful presentation, don't simply plant your bulbs in bare soil. The blooms will be getting the most attention, but the full visual effect will be heightened if you treat each pot like a little garden: Sow annual ryegrass seeds around the base for a tiny meadow, or decorate the soil surface with moss. Stage pots in groupings rather than alone for the most drama. And don't overlook their possibilities as cut flowers: If you can bear it, sacrifice some long stems and create impressive, lush arrangements with the spectacular blooms. What could make a nicer holiday centerpiece—especially in a festive, Christmas red?

AMARYLLIS GLOSSARY

1. *'Desert Dawn'* is a Christmas-flowering variety with fourteen- to sixteen-inch stems. 2. *'Springtime'* is a soft rose-pink shaded over white. It takes about six weeks to bloom after planting. 3. *'Baby Star'* is a miniature type with red-and-white striped flowers. 4. *'Carnival,'* its white petals striped with red, evokes a Christmas candy cane. 5. *'Candy Floss'* bears deep-pink flowers on sturdy stems. 6. *'Spotty,'* a slender, vigorous amaryllis, can grow to twenty-six inches or taller. 7. *'Summertime'* blooms four to six weeks after planting. 8. *'Lady Jane'* is a double-flowered Dutch hybrid. The Dutch hybrids take six to twelve weeks to flower after being potted. 9. *'Double Record,'* another Dutch hybrid, is white with red shading. 10. *'Scarlet Baby'* is a miniature variety, with brilliant-red, well-proportioned flowers. 11. *'Rainbow'* is a picotee variety, meaning it has a delicate, darker edge to the petals. 12. *'Bolero'* takes about ten weeks to bloom. 13. *'Wedding Dance,'* a Christmas-flowering variety, has glistening white, star-shaped flowers. 14. *'Pamela'* is a miniature variety, with rosy-red flowers. 15. *'Minerva,'* a Dutch hybrid, has large, six-inch flowers on sixteen- to eighteen-inch stems. 16. *'Milady'* produces large pink flowers four to six weeks after potting.

Nᴼ. 1 *Desert Dawn*

Nᴼ. 2 *Springtime*

Nᴼ. 3 *Baby Star*

Nᴼ. 4 *Carnival*

Nᴼ. 5 *Candy Floss*

Nᴼ. 6 *Spotty*

Nᴼ. 7 *Summertime*

Nᴼ. 8 *Lady Jane*

Nᴼ. 9 *Double Record*

Nᴼ. 10 *Scarlet Baby*

Nᴼ. 11 *Rainbow*

Nᴼ. 12 *Bolero*

Nᴼ. 13 *Wedding Dance*

Nᴼ. 14 *Pamela*

Nᴼ. 15 *Minerva*

Nᴼ. 16 *Milady*

AMARYLLIS DISPLAYS CLOCKWISE FROM TOP LEFT: *Two bulbs of* Hippeastrum *'Green Goddess' flank a picotee amaryllis in an intricate cast iron planter. For simple hostess gifts, tuck bulbs into painted terra-cotta pots; use double-sided tape to attach ribbon around pot rims, and tie on a handwritten gift tag. Draw attention to the amaryllis's showy flower by cutting down overwhelming stalks. Arrange shortened blooms (choose varieties in reds and whites), along with gooseneck loosestrife, in small vessels; set between place settings.* OPPOSITE: *Two square terra-cotta pots are painted white and filled with Spanish moss (whitened from a light dusting of spray snow), making airy homes for H. 'Green Goddess.'*

LIVING COLOR *A partially shaded window supplies the bright, indirect light in which* Schlumbergera *thrives. The plant hanger cradles* S. *'White Christmas.'* OPPOSITE: *These four antique lamp brackets hold* Schlumbergera *in pastels that harmonize with the whites of the buffet and sconce. The plants paired at top are hybrids; below are 'Lavender Doll' twins, and in the mirrored container, 'Pink Pearl.'*

PRUNING AND PROPAGATING

YOU WILL NEED *floral shears * sharp knife * fast-draining potting mix * rooting hormone * three-inch pots*

1. After a Christmas cactus has finished flowering, give it a light pruning: With your thumb and index finger, twist off segments from the stem ends, or snip them with shears. **2.** Repotting is rarely necessary, but plants should be rejuvenated every few years. Remove the plant from its pot, then use a knife to score the outside of the root ball in three or four places, and make V-shape cuts about one inch deep. Replace the plant in the container, and insert fast-draining potting mix into the cuts, tamping the soil lightly with a stick or a pencil. **3.** To propagate cuttings: After the flowers have faded, clip off two to three stem segments (ideally each cutting should have several branches). Dip cut end into rooting hormone, available at garden centers, then leave it on a work surface for two to three days so the cut can callous over. **4.** Plant the cuttings in fast-draining potting mix, putting two or three cuttings in each three-inch pot. Place them where they will receive filtered, indirect light; keep the potting mix evenly moist. Working a year in advance, this is a simple way to make holiday gifts.

FESTIVE TRIMMINGS OPPOSITE: *Three pots of mature S. 'Christmas Fantasy' preside at the center of a holiday table; cuttings from that trio serve as place markers and party favors.* RIGHT: *Set in green cachepots to unify the theme for a gathering of* Schlumbergera *cultivars, these rain-forest natives bring extra warmth to a fireplace strung with North American evergreens. 'Kris Kringle' and 'Christmas Charm' glow atop a pedestal table before the hearth. The mantel supports 'Peach Parfait,' 'Pinkie,' 'Lavender Girl,' and other varieties.*

FRUITCAKE

a neglected art

✳

There was a time when fruitcake was synonymous with Christmas generosity and goodwill. The finest ingredients were gathered and lovingly tended according to time-honored family recipes; and the cakes—filled with gem-colored candied fruits and nuts, and soaked in liquor—were culinary decadence at its best. Why, then, has fruitcake been dropped from our holiday wish lists?

The explanation lies in the ingredients: In recent years, many people have started taking shortcuts with their fruitcakes, using store-bought fruit mixtures that are mostly green cherries and pre-chopped, artificially colored citrus peels. The nuts, when there are any, are usually old and, worse, rancid, and fine liquor or liqueur such as brandy or dry sherry is often replaced with something akin to grenadine. The result, unfortunately, is a heavy, sticky-sweet, unpalatable mess.

Thankfully, it doesn't have to be that way. Fruitcake can be scrumptious when baked with the high-quality fruits and nuts you love, in your favorite combinations. Select your ingredients and plan well ahead: Bake the cakes at least a month, if not two or three, before they will be eaten, then allow them to age and ferment, dousing them weekly in liquor to preserve them.

Whatever your negative notions about fruitcake, at least one of the recipes in this book will change your mind. Give it a try. You may find that baking fruitcake becomes one of your favorite holiday rituals. And all the lucky people on your gift list will be happier for it.

FIVE VARIETIES *Don't miss out on fruitcake—there is a recipe for everyone.* FROM TOP TO BOTTOM: *Dowager Duchess Fruitcake, Backhouse Family Fruitcake (one kitchen staffer's traditional version), Chocolate Panforte, Fruit and Stout Cake, and Figgy Christmas Fruit Roll.*

THE PROCESS ABOVE, FROM LEFT: *This dried and candied fruit, beautifully cut, is nothing like the sticky, pre-chopped mixtures sold in stores. Alcohol (rum shown here) preserves fruitcakes; mixing with the fruit, it starts fermentation, creating that wonderful taste that only improves with time. Wrap cakes in muslin or cheesecloth, and set aside to ripen for a month before serving. Attach cards to the cakes so you can keep track of each time you bless them with liquor.* RIGHT: *Fruit and Stout Cake, spread with a rich creamy cheese, and Dowager Duchess Fruitcake turn into a little meal with the addition of fresh pears and clementines.* OPPOSITE: *Fill your fruitcake with ingredients you love. Gather all your ingredients together before you start. Test to see if your selected fruits and nuts work together before making any decisions. Just pop a small handful into your mouth. The cakes are forgiving; you can substitute one fruit or nut for almost any other in each recipe. It's important to have a balance of tastes and textures, such as chewy and crunchy or sweet and tart.*

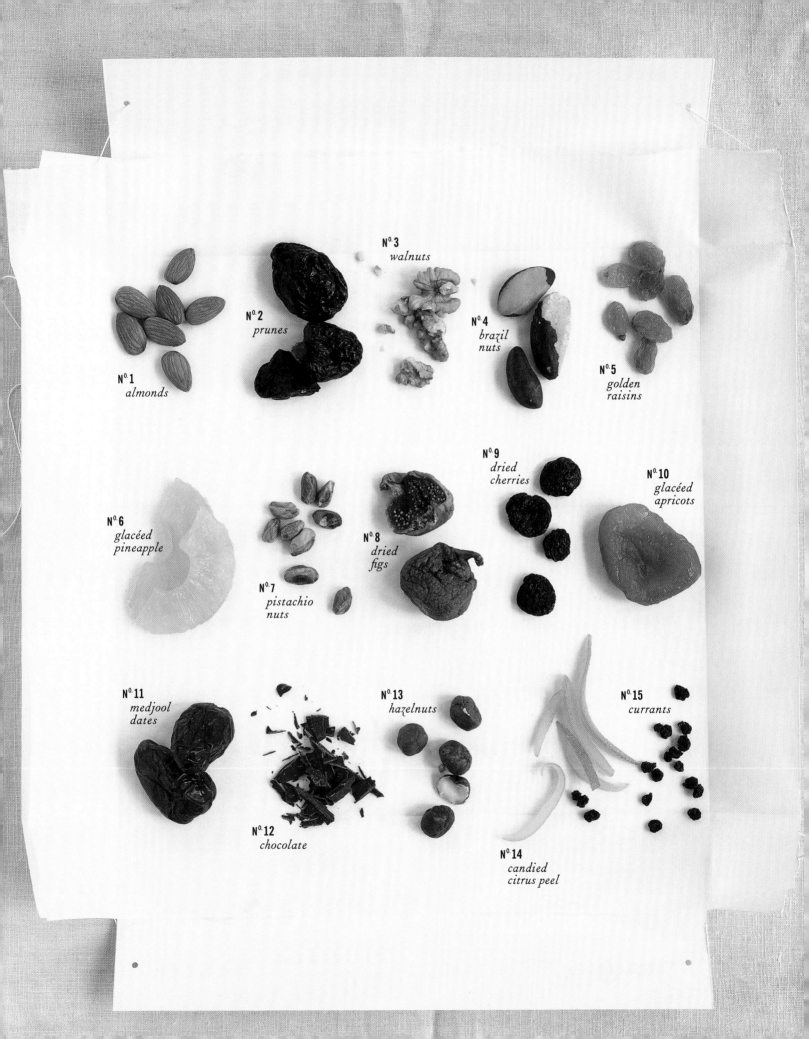

N⁰.3
walnuts

N⁰.2
prunes

N⁰.4
*brazil
nuts*

N⁰.1
almonds

N⁰.5
*golden
raisins*

N⁰.9
*dried
cherries*

N⁰.10
*glacéed
apricots*

N⁰.6
*glacéed
pineapple*

N⁰.8
*dried
figs*

N⁰.7
*pistachio
nuts*

N⁰.11
*medjool
dates*

N⁰.13
hazelnuts

N⁰.15
currants

N⁰.12
chocolate

N⁰.14
*candied
citrus peel*

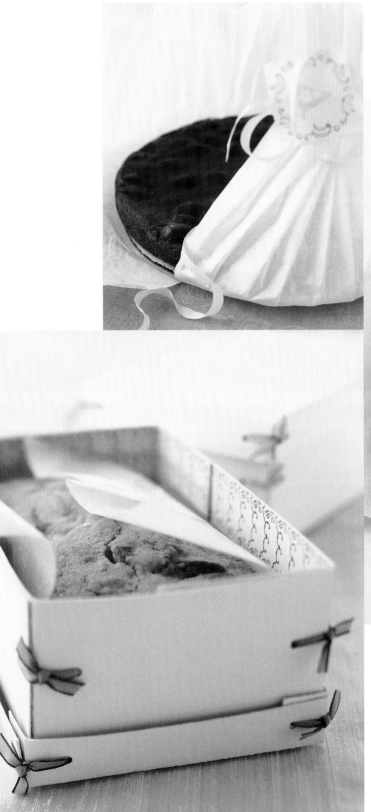

PRETTY PACKAGING *Fruitcakes are labors of love and deserve gorgeous packaging.* OPPOSITE: *A box made out of poster board covered with decorative paper holds a rectangular cake perfectly. Wrap round flat cakes, such as panforte, in onion skin or parchment paper. Crepe paper and ribbon made from sequins strung whimsically on metallic thread also make good wrapping.* THIS PAGE, CLOCKWISE FROM TOP LEFT: *Chocolate Panforte does not need to age much. Figgy Christmas Fruit Roll is wrapped in edible rice paper instead of muslin. Dowager Duchess Fruitcake peeks out of its handmade box.*

SEE THE RECIPES

love and joy
at Christmastime
and throughout
the new year
the Reeds

Merry
Christmas
Violet
love,
Gracie xo.

MR. *and* MRS. MAUS'S
FRUITCAKE

I think about Mr. and Mrs. Robert Maus a lot. They were our jolly German-born neighbors who lived right next door to our house at 86 Elm Place. Retired bakers, having sold their profitable bakery in Newark, New Jersey, they were anything but retired from their art. Still enamored of flour and sugar and butter and cream and fresh and dried fruits and nuts, they transformed, little by little, their concrete-floored basement into a mini version of their former professional premises. Wooden tables, fat legged and sturdy, had unpainted tops that were silken and smooth to the touch, reflecting years and years of kneading doughs and rolling pastries. The ovens were not like ours next door, a small gas wall unit that could barely hold a family-size turkey, but large "professional" ranges, black with age. The floor felt as soft as the tops of the work tables, surely the result of flour and sugar sanding its surface year after year. * From my perspective—that of a young child—everything seemed larger than life, although my mother assures me that everything was just larger than I was used to, starting with the Mauses themselves. They were not like any other acquaintances. I always thought of them as fairy-tale characters, just as the children's book author Maurice Sendak envisions the bakers in his famous *In the Night Kitchen*. * Despite their retirement, the Mauses baked as if they had customers lined up at the front door. They were always experimenting and trying new recipes and ideas, using age-old techniques they had acquired in Germany, where they had apprenticed under a "natural" master baker who used only the best ingredients, with fabulous results. Thus the Danish pastries that emerged from those big ovens on full sheet pans, dented and blackened around the edges from many years of use, were delicate and flaky and filled with sweet apricots and prunes and apples, not out of cans, but fresh and plump. * There were no mixers in the basement bakery: Everything was stirred and kneaded and mixed by hand. Mr. Maus would tell me over and over that that was why his cakes were lighter, his breads higher, his creams fluffier, and his pastries flakier. To this day I believe him and use his instructions when I bake or cook. His yeast doughs would rise in the enveloping warmth of the big oil furnace that heated his house. He used large yellowware bowls that Mrs. Maus lovingly cared for—there were no cracks or chips in those bowls. Thin, well-washed linen towels were used to cover the doughs, and pans of water were placed here and there in the cellar to create the "humidity" that Mr. Maus knew was essential to the tenderness of a fine yeast bread. His rolling pins were immense—longer and bigger than any

I had ever seen, and when I was a young housewife buying my own baking tools, I looked for the same kinds of giant wooden rolling pins and steel pans and heavy tin molds that the Mauses used. I still have and cherish one of their yellowware bowls, which

Dense and rich, garnished with apricots and pecan halves, Mr. and Mrs. Maus's fruitcake brings back memories from childhood holidays at the very first bite. Their recipe is foolproof, and it's still the one I use myself, year after year.

I use for rising my mother's babka dough. ∗ Perhaps the most memorable of the Mauses' creations, and one that we still

make in our family, is their fruitcake. It's rich and heavy and dark. As with any good fruitcake, you must use the best-quality dried fruits and candied fruits you can find; I spend a day just gathering my ingredients. Then everything must be chopped by hand, pans and tins must be lined with buttered brown paper or heavy waxed paper, and the cakes must be baked for about three and a half hours in a bain-marie. ∗ Look for the fruitcake in The Recipes. It's a Christmas gift to you from me and Mr. and Mrs. Maus. ∗ *Martha Stewart*

CITRUS

fresh colors and flavors

*

Imagine an icy Christmas morning in England a century ago: A child reaches into his stocking to find a single orange in the toe. It is a perfect little package of sunshine and sweetness, too precious for any other day of the year. Citrus fruit was once a rare commodity for anyone not living in a tropical climate; many people reserved it, like other luxury items, for the most special of occasions. Today, of course, all types of citrus fruits are available in abundance, especially in the winter months. As symbols of the holiday season, however, they still possess a certain magic.

Citrus fruits grow in a brilliant palette of tropical shades, offering a pleasant variation on the classic Christmas reds and golds; they can fill a room with marvelous fragrance; and their refresh-ing flavors nicely balance the rich foods we prepare for holiday dinners. The shapes of the fruits lend themselves to decorating projects, as well. You can carve their rinds into patterns and pile them into bowls as sunny centerpieces, or scoop them out and make natural votive candles. Take a look at the produce section of your local market. The old standbys—navel oranges, ruby-red grapefruit, lemons, and limes—are represented, of course, but there are many more exotic choices, including red-violet blood oranges, tiny kumquat hybrids, and big, tender pommelos. All have unique ornamental and culinary possibilities. Add a few touches to brighten a room, or let the sunny tropical theme define your holiday decorating. Every Christmas doesn't have to be white.

CITRUS PUNCH FROM LEFT: *Planter's Punch (made with rum and lemon, lime, orange, and pineapple juices) is kept cold by frozen citrus, added just before serving. Frozen clove-spiked lemon "ice cubes" cool a bowl of Iced Spice Tea. A simple chilled rosé rounds out the offerings.*

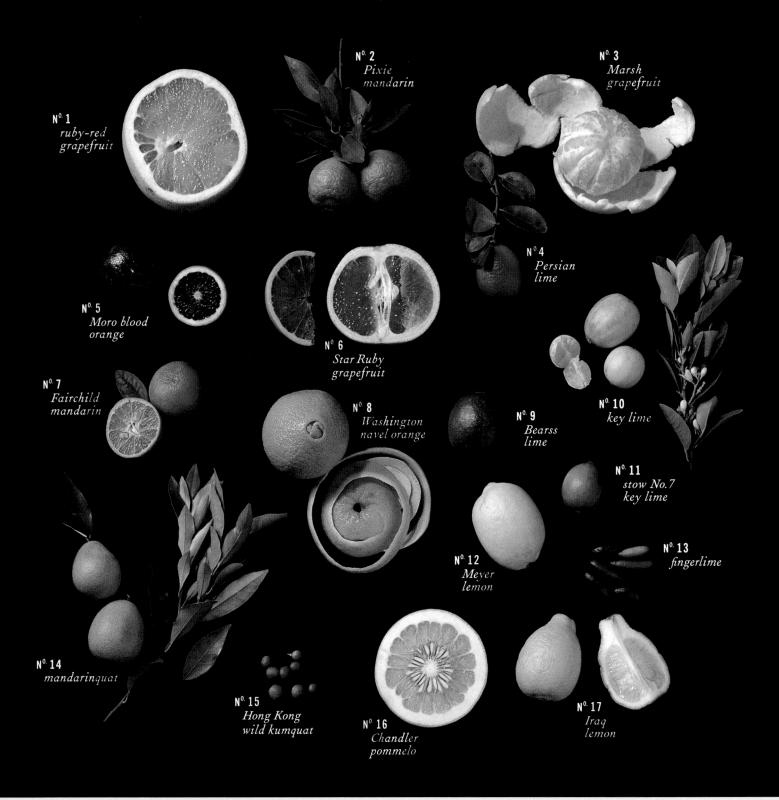

N⁰. 1 *ruby-red grapefruit*

N⁰. 2 *Pixie mandarin*

N⁰. 3 *Marsh grapefruit*

N⁰. 4 *Persian lime*

N⁰. 5 *Moro blood orange*

N⁰. 6 *Star Ruby grapefruit*

N⁰. 7 *Fairchild mandarin*

N⁰. 8 *Washington navel orange*

N⁰. 9 *Bearss lime*

N⁰. 10 *key lime*

N⁰. 11 *stow No. 7 key lime*

N⁰. 12 *Meyer lemon*

N⁰. 13 *fingerlime*

N⁰. 14 *mandarinquat*

N⁰. 15 *Hong Kong wild kumquat*

N⁰. 16 *Chandler pommelo*

N⁰. 17 *Iraq lemon*

CITRUS GLOSSARY *The flesh of ruby-red grapefruit* (1) *comes in a range of pinks. The Pixie mandarin* (2, 18) *is seedless and easy to peel. Among the most common white-fleshed grapefruits is the Marsh grapefruit* (3, 27). *The large-fruited Persian lime* (4) *is typically Florida-grown. The Moro blood orange* (5), *an Italian variety, has juicy red-violet flesh. The Texas-grown Star Ruby grapefruit* (6) *has deep-red fruit. The Fairchild mandarin* (7) *is an offspring of the clementine, a sweet holiday standard. The Washington navel* (8) *is widely held to be the best eating orange. The Bearss lime* (9) *has large, yellow-green fruit. Key limes* (10, 11), *sometimes called Mexican limes, are small-fruited and aromatic. The Meyer lemon* (12) *is a sweet, mild-flavored hybrid. The unusual fingerlime* (13), *native only to Australia, has a very sour taste. The mandarinquat* (14) *is a mandarin orange–kumquat hybrid. The tiny Hong Kong wild kumquat* (15)

Nº 18
*Pixie
mandarin*

Nº 19
*Eureka
lemon*

Nº 20
*Meiwa
kumquat*

Nº 21
*Chandler
pommelo*

Nº 22
*variegated
"pink lemonade"
lemon*

Nº 23
*sectored
orange*

Nº 24
calamondin

Nº 26
*Nagami
kumquat*

Nº 25
procimequat

Nº 27
*Marsh
grapefruit*

Nº 28
tangelo

Nº 29
*vainiglia
orange*

Nº 30
citron

is a popular ornamental. Slightly larger than a grapefruit, the Chandler pommelo (**16, 21**) has tart, firm flesh; pommelos are ancestors to grapefruit. The Iraq lemon (**17**) has a knobby end. The Eureka lemon (**19**) is very juicy and has few seeds. The Meiwa kumquat (**20**) is round with a sweet rind. The variegated "pink lemonade" lemon (**22**) is a pink-fleshed cousin to the Eureka. The extremely rare sectored orange (**23**) has an unusually variegated rind. Both the calamondin (**24**) and procimequat (**25**) are kumquat hybrids. The foliage of the oval-shaped Nagami kumquat (**26**) makes it a desirable potted plant; its fruit is typically used for preserves. The tangelo (**28**) is a delicious, if unattractive, cross between the tangerine, grapefruit, and orange. The vainiglia acidless pink orange (**29**) has a sweet, bland flavor. The citron (**30**), which looks like a huge lemon, is sour, dry, and fragrant; it is not eaten raw, but its peel is candied for baking.

CARVING CITRUS

YOU WILL NEED *assorted citrus fruits ∗ linoleum cutter with V-shape and square blades*

The tender, colorful rinds of citrus fruits peel away to reveal the soft, white pith beneath, lending themselves to cutouts. Using a standard linoleum cutter with a V-shape blade, available in craft and hardware stores, you can easily carve flower petals and other shapes. It may take a bit of practice to achieve the appropriate depth of cut for each variety of fruit. To make spiral cuts, a tool with a square blade will yield a more even pattern. For the prettiest and freshest presentation, make these designs on the day you plan to display the fruit.

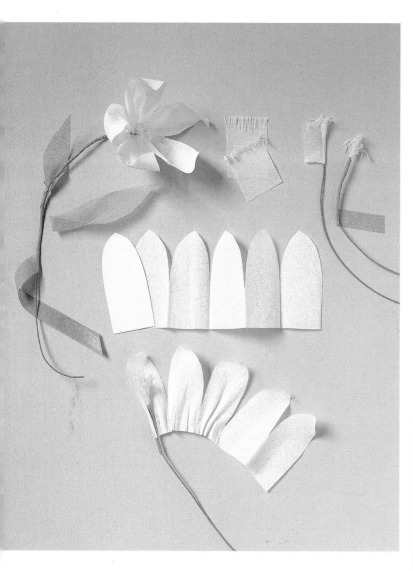

CREPE-PAPER ORANGE BLOSSOMS

YOU WILL NEED *photocopier ∗ white, yellow, and green crepe paper ∗ cloth-covered floral wire ∗ floral tape*

Photocopy templates on page 134, enlarging 200 percent for large, and 150 percent for smaller blossoms. Accordion-fold white crepe paper into width of template. Place template on top, and trace flower petal template onto paper. Trace stamen onto yellow paper and leaves onto green paper. The paper grain should run vertically on patterns. Cut out shapes. Gently curl ends of petals on scissors. Use scissors to fringe-cut ends of stamen; wrap ends around a pencil to curl. Tightly wrap stamen around end of a length of floral wire, then secure by wrapping with floral tape. Unfold the accordion-folded petals, and wrap them around the stamen at top of wire, pleating bottom edge of petals as you go so petals are evenly spaced and don't overlap. Wrap base of petals with more floral tape. As you wind tape down the stem, pinch the bottom of a green crepe-paper leaf, attach it to stem, and continue taping. Fluff petals.

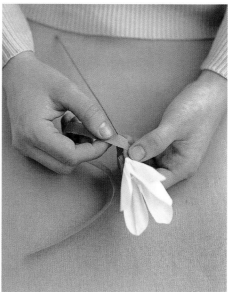

CITRUS DISPLAY *A two-tiered glass compote is piled high with oranges, blood oranges, lemons, and limes—all decorated with carved designs. Tiny kumquats fill the base of each dish, supporting the larger fruit and anchoring the paper blossoms that complete the arrangement. The colorful compote attracts hungry guests to the hors d'oeuvres table, where a platter of star-shaped gravlax canapés awaits.*

CITRUS TREE *Glittered fruit, light paper blossoms, and butterflies, inspired by traditional Chinese paper crafts are a sunny twist on customary holiday decorations. Red candles (for decoration, not burning) add an old-fashioned touch. Moss "tree skirt," shaped by a chicken-wire armature on a plastic tarp, should be kept moist.*

BUTTERFLIES

YOU WILL NEED *photocopier • crepe paper • metallic paint pen • paintbrushes • flat clothespins • water-based sizing • mica powders • 18-gauge floral wire*

Photocopy butterfly templates on page 134, enlarging 200 percent. Trace shapes onto crepe paper with grain running horizontally; cut out. Outline edges with a metallic paint pen. Brush clothespins with sizing; let dry until tacky, then brush on mica powders. Let dry completely. Stack together two butterfly shapes in different sizes and colors. Slide crepe paper into center of clothespin, gathering crepe. For hanger, wrap wire around neck of clothespin; fluff wings.

GLITTERED FRUIT

YOU WILL NEED *plastic fruits • stiff wire or skewer • sponge paintbrush • craft glue • coarse glass glitter • floral foam • narrow ribbon • half-inch straight pins • metallic thread • beads and sequins*

Plastic fruits with foam centers work well for this project. Poke the end of a length of stiff wire into fruit; while holding wire, sponge-brush fruit with craft glue, then gently roll fruit in coarse glass glitter, using a spoon to cover all surfaces. Poke the end of the wire into a block of floral foam, so that fruit stays upright without touching any surface while glue and glitter dry. Once fruit is dry, cross two twelve-inch lengths of narrow ribbon at the bottom, and secure with a straight pin. Bring pieces of ribbon up and around fruit; pin together at top, tying ends into a loop to serve as a hanger. If desired, embellish ornaments with glittery, metallic thread, as well as beads and sequins, secured with more straight pins.

CITRUSY BUFFET *The bright, tangy flavors of citrus fruits complement the rich fare typically served over the holidays. For this dinner, a simple roasted pork loin is transformed into a sophisticated offering after it has been marinated overnight in a blend of honey, vinegar, olive oil, shallots, and cinnamon. An aromatic orange, fig, and prune stuffing is cooked inside the butterflied loin. Side dishes include endive braised in chicken stock with star anise and garnished with sweet, acidless pink oranges; and a salad of ruby-red grapefruit, blood oranges, and navel oranges with peel and pith removed (you can use any juicy citrus that is fresh at the market). The fruit is arranged on a bed of frisée, topped with toasted hazelnuts, and drizzled with Lemon-Cream Vinaigrette.*

LEMON CANDLES

YOU WILL NEED *beeswax • coloring chips • waxed paper • lemons • all-cotton wicks • metal wick holders*

Make lemon candles on the day you plan to use them, since rinds dry out and pull away from wax. Melt beeswax (it burns more slowly than paraffin) in top of a double-boiler. If desired, color wax by adding coloring chips (found at candle-making-supply stores), one at a time. Test color: Spoon hot wax onto waxed paper, and let cool. Once desired color is achieved, cut lemons in half lengthwise, and remove pulp. Place rinds on waxed paper, and secure wicks in their centers with wick holders. Carefully fill with melted wax; let set for thirty minutes. Trim wick to one-quarter inch before burning. You might want to place a dish beneath candles in case of spills.

FRESH HOLIDAY FLAVORS CLOCKWISE, FROM TOP LEFT: *A citrus smoothie is an easy and refreshing alternative to a rich Christmas-morning breakfast; to make, layer orange and pineapple slush with banana-cinnamon yogurt, and top with an orange slice. A simple glazed Citrus Cake is garnished with thin strips of candied orange peel. Candied orange and lemon peels preserved in sugar syrup— tied with bows and hand-labeled—make great gifts. They're good for toppings. You can also dip them in chocolate or roll them in sugar for a candy bowl.*

CITRUS DESSERTS *Lime-Cornmeal Glazed Cookies make a satisfying, not-too-sweet ending to a meal. Our airy Lemon-Chiffon Cake is topped with a juicy, colorful compote of blood oranges, navel oranges, and ruby-red grapefruit.* SEE THE RECIPES

LEAVES

velvety details

Leaves are a little like snowflakes: Each is a marvel of structure and design, and no two, it seems, are precisely alike. Whether they spiral to the ground in vivid colors each fall or cling, gracefully evergreen, to branches year-round—their beauty is both remarkable and ephemeral. Bring a leaf inside, weave it into a wreath or an arrangement of seasonal blooms, and its character changes: Its rich colors begin to fade, and its supple texture gradually becomes dry and brittle.

To decorate with leaves, then, requires capturing their essence in an enduring form. The projects you'll discover on the following pages are intended to do just that. You can gather up your favorite leaves in autumn, and then use their shapes as inspiration for your holiday designs. Transfer them onto wrapping paper, gift cards, and tags; or use our leaf templates to create rubber stamps and emboss the shapes onto rich, luscious velvet.

For our velvet leaf projects, we chose a silk-rayon blend because its long fibers and dense pile make it easy to emboss. When a rubber stamp is pressed against the velvet with an iron, the heat engraves the pattern onto the fabric. Spend an afternoon making an assortment of leaves in this fashion, then use them as luxurious trimmings for stockings, gifts, and Christmas ornaments; or wire them together to form elegant wreaths and garlands. All will last nicely through the holiday season. Afterward, store them away until the next year, and bring them out again when the last leaves have fallen from the trees.

VELVET LEAF STOCKINGS *Small packages spill from a pair of soft, voluminous stockings decorated with velvet holly leaves, which were embossed using an ordinary iron and a rubber stamp. For embossing instructions, see page 82; for the stocking template and instructions, see page 136.*

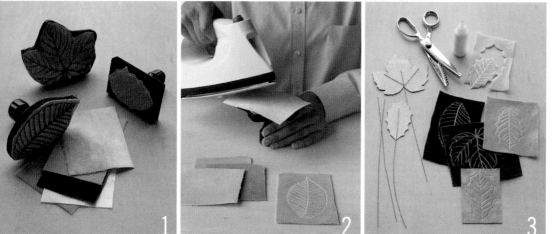

EMBOSSING VELVET

YOU WILL NEED *photocopier * rubber stamps * velvet * iron-on cotton interfacing * iron * pinking shears * eighteen-gauge and smaller-gauge floral wire * craft glue * ribbon * "Yes" glue*

Nearly all the projects in this chapter begin with leaves made using this process. Photocopy leaf templates on page 135, sizing as indicated or as desired; cut out, and have them made into rubber stamps at an office-supply store (see The Guide). The velvet needs to be interfaced to make it sturdy and to prevent fraying. Use white or black single-sided, medium-weight, iron-on cotton interfacing. **1.** Cut a piece of interfacing about half an inch larger on all sides than the leaf stamp. Cut a piece of velvet the same size; set it fuzzy-side down. Place interfacing on back of velvet, shiny-side down. **2.** With iron on medium-high heat, press the two fabrics together for five to ten seconds to fuse. Lay interfaced fabric, velvet side down, on top of stamp. Spray interfacing with water. With a hot iron, press fabric for ten to fifteen seconds, using firm circular motions, to scorch the stamp into the velvet. **3.** Cut out leaf shapes (use pinking shears for birch leaves). Give leaves for a garland or wreath long stems (six or seven inches), leaves for tree ornaments short stems; stocking and pillow-trim leaves have no stems at all. Make stems from floral wire: eighteen-gauge wire for larger leaves, smaller-gauge for smaller leaves. Affix a length of wire to back of each leaf with craft glue, starting about half an inch from top. For wide leaves, branch wire at top by twisting a shorter piece around stem. **4.** Sew a few stitches on the back of each leaf where floral wire and bottom of leaf meet to secure stem. **5.** For each bird, make two matching squares of interfaced velvet. Emboss one with bird shape. For hanger, first cut notch at top of that outline; affix ribbon loop to back of bird with "Yes" glue. Coat entire back of embossed velvet panel with "Yes" glue, press to plain interfaced panel, sandwiching ribbon hanger. Cut out bird.

VELVET LEAF GLOSSARY *We have provided templates (see page 135) for each of these leaves, many of which you'll recognize from your own autumn collections. Birds are natural complements for the leaf theme. Use field guides to render your own favorite species in velvet.*

Nº. 1
maple

Nº. 2
birch

Nº. 3
holly

Nº. 4
chickadee

Nº. 5
fig

Nº. 6
poplar

Nº. 7
mistletoe

Nº. 8
grape

Nº. 9
oak

Nº. 10
nuthatch

Nº. 11
dove

Nº. 12
sassafras

Nº. 13
ginkgo

HOLLY GARLAND

YOU WILL NEED *long-stemmed velvet holly leaves • eight-millimeter silver beads • eighteen-gauge nickel wire • floral tape • pushpins*

One of the most graceful ways to evoke the holiday season is to drape a hand-crafted garland over a mirror or mantel. To make a seven-foot garland, you'll need an assortment of small and large long-stemmed velvet holly leaves (we used about one hundred and sixty in various shades of silvery green) and about eighty-four silver beads. First, make the holly-berry bunches—there are three berries in each bunch. Make four bundles for every foot of garland. Cut an eight-inch length of nickel wire, and thread it through a silver bead so bead is centered on wire; twist wires together from top. Repeat with two more wires; twist all wires together to form a bunch. Next, working downward, layer stems of holly leaves on top of each other, randomly alternating small and large leaves. Tightly wrap stems with floral tape to secure as you go. Add a bunch of berries every three inches, wrapping it with floral tape as well. Continue layering and taping until garland has reached desired length. Drape garland into a swag; hang with pushpins.

VELVET LEAF PILLOW

YOU WILL NEED *linen • pillow insert • photocopier • transfer paper • velvet mistletoe leaves without stems and dove • green embroidery floss • sewing machine • pearly beads • gold cording*

Cut two squares of linen to pillow insert size plus a quarter inch for seam. Photo-copy template on page 136, enlarging as needed. Put transfer paper between template and one linen square; pin in place. Trace design onto linen with pencil (right). Make leaves and dove from templates on page 135 according to technique on page 82; cut just outside perimeter to allow for stitching. Pin leaves and dove into place on linen; create stems and branches (far right) with embroidery floss and chain stitch (see page 136 for diagram). Machine-stitch leaves and dove onto linen. Sew on one or two beads between leaves. Pin linen panels right-sides together; machine-stitch three sides. Turn right side out, insert pillow; hand-stitch closed. Hand-stitch cording to pillow.

LEAFY LINEN PILLOW *A dove, framed by sprays of mistletoe on this simple linen pillow, symbolizes the season of peace. The velvet leaves and corded trim provide luxurious details.*

HOLIDAY KEEPSAKES *Embossed-velvet leaves and birds lend themselves to countless crafts: Use them to accessorize a glasses case (see page 137 for instructions) or jewelry box, or to make elegant bookmarks.* OPPOSITE: *Ornamental greenery fades, but a wreath rendered in velvet will last for many a season. See page 88 for instructions.*

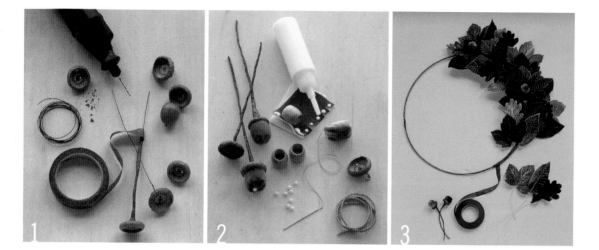

VELVET LEAF WREATH

YOU WILL NEED *long-stemmed velvet leaves · acorns · Dremel drill · twenty-four-gauge floral wire · brown floral tape · wooden beads · velvet · craft glue · small beads or faux pearls · fourteen-inch, single-wire wreath form*

A holiday wreath can be fashioned from velvet leaves in various shades of red and pink (as on page 87), or in elegant golden hues for an especially lustrous effect. Begin with a selection of maple, birch, and oak leaves, as well as some velvet-covered acorns. For a fourteen-inch, single-wire wreath form, we used about eighty-five leaves and about fif-

teen acorns. **1.** To make velvet acorns: Pull off an acorn's cap. Drill two holes in cap. Cut a ten-inch length of floral wire; pass it through both holes so ends come out of cap top. Twist wire ends together. Starting where wire meets cap, wrap wire with floral tape. **2.** Select a wooden bead that fits loosely into cap. Cut a small rectangle of velvet large enough to cover circumference of bead, allowing extra fabric at both ends. Cut five or six small notches into velvet where it will cover one end of bead. Dot notches and ends of velvet with glue. Roll velvet around bead. Fold down notches to cover bead end (this

end will be covered by cap). Sew a running stitch at other end, cinch closed, and sew a small bead or faux pearl on top. Glue covered bead into cap. **3.** For wreath: Working clockwise, attach a few leaves at a time to wreath form, securing with a few tight twists of floral tape around stems. Layer leaves so they cover about half of each leaf that precedes them. Angle leaves by bending stems so they don't lie flat; this will give wreath a natural-looking fullness. To hide stems of the last leaves attached, tuck them beneath those first wired into place. To finish, weave acorns into wreath.

LEAF WRAPPING AND PAPER CARDS

YOU WILL NEED *pressed leaves · lightweight craft paper · crayon · eraser · velvet paper · rubber stamps · iron · PMA adhesive · card stock · ribbon*

Gathered and pressed in the fall, a collection of leaves can be used to adorn holiday gift papers. **1.** For wrapping paper, place leaves, vein side up, on work surface, and cover with smooth, lightweight craft paper in color of choice. Rub lightly over leaf with crayon, revealing its shape; use eraser to clean up any errant marks. **2.** To make cards, place fuzzy side of velvet paper over a rubber stamp, and press with a medium-hot iron from the other side; hold for several seconds. Press a sheet of PMA adhesive to back of embossed paper; burnish, and remove to leave a sticky surface. Press paper onto a piece of folded card stock, with part of the outline touching the fold. Cut out card, leaving folded joint intact. Attach with ribbon to presents wrapped in leaf-printed paper.

WINTER BERRIES

decorative harvest

✳

They are the plump, colorful dazzlers of the winter garden. Even some of their names—beautyberry, firethorn, bittersweet—hint at their star status. Used sparingly in displays of holiday greenery, winter berries are accommodating, providing just a sparkle of vivid color. But given the chance in lush wreaths and delicate, twining garlands, they will seize the spotlight themselves, even without the benefit of evergreens.

Berries are a staple food for birds during the winter months and are much more plentiful, and common, than you might imagine. There are species that do well in nearly every climate. Some grow in eye-popping clusters against dark foliage; others lurk beneath leaves in soft, transparent blues, greens, and silvery-whites. All are worth seeking out. Don't feel guilty about harvesting them from your yard—many bushes and trees need a good pruning every year anyway; just be careful to consider each plant's well-being. In the case of mistletoe, which is actually a parasite that grows high in treetops, harvesting is necessary to keep it from overwhelming your trees. If you lack berries in your yard, visit a local florist; most carry ornamental winter berries—such as holly and dried pepperberries—around the holiday season.

As with all plants, use caution when displaying winter berries. Many—mistletoe, holly, and bittersweet, to name a few—are toxic if ingested by humans or pets. Birds sing a different tune: Hang a winter-berry wreath outside, and they will have a holiday feast beyond their wildest dreams.

RING OF BERRIES *Rich colors and textures give this lush wreath a deceptively complex appearance. It is made of bundles of only three kinds of berries. The tiny deep-red clusters are sumac; the orange-red berries are firethorn, and the large apricot-hued berries are from the strawberry tree.*

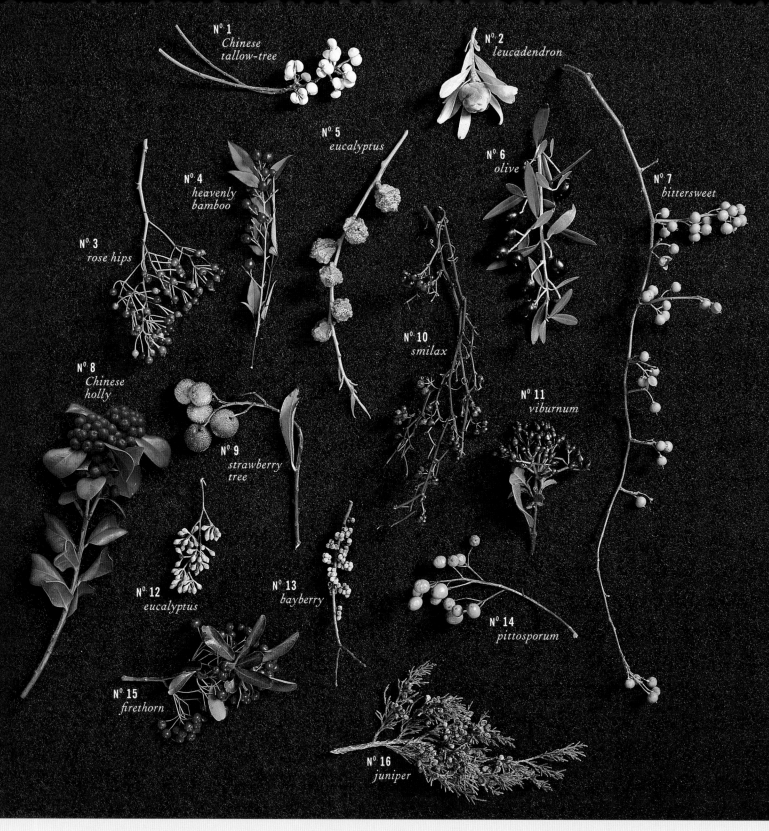

N°. 1
Chinese tallow-tree

N°. 2
leucadendron

N°. 5
eucalyptus

N°. 6
olive

N°. 7
bittersweet

N°. 4
heavenly bamboo

N°. 3
rose hips

N°. 10
smilax

N°. 8
Chinese holly

N°. 11
viburnum

N°. 9
strawberry tree

N°. 12
eucalyptus

N°. 13
bayberry

N°. 14
pittosporum

N°. 15
firethorn

N°. 16
juniper

WINTER BERRY GLOSSARY Sapium sebiferum, *or Chinese tallow-tree* **(1)**, *produces vividly white fruit.* Leucadendron, *with fruit ranging from silver to red* **(2, 30, 31, 32)**, *are commonly grown in the Southwest. Rose hips* **(3)**, *the fruit of the rose plant, appear once the flowers die off and stay throughout winter. The red-berried* Nandina domestica, *or heavenly bamboo* **(4)**, *is a popular broadleaf evergreen. If eucalyptus* **(5, 12, 24)** *is not hardy in your area, check a local florist's shop. Smilax* **(10)** *is a thorny climbing vine. The* Olea europaea, *or olive* **(6)**, *has visual as well as culinary appeal. The twining vines of* Celastrus, *or bittersweet* **(7)**, *produce bright yellow and red fruit.* Ilex cornuta 'Bufordii,' *a Chinese holly* **(8)**, *bears fruit without pollination. Common in California gardens,* Arbutus unedo, *the strawberry tree* **(9)**, *yields large tough-skinned berries. Viburnum* **(11)** *is a warm-climate broadleaf evergreen that has blue-black fruit. An East Coast native,* Myrica pensylvanica, *or*

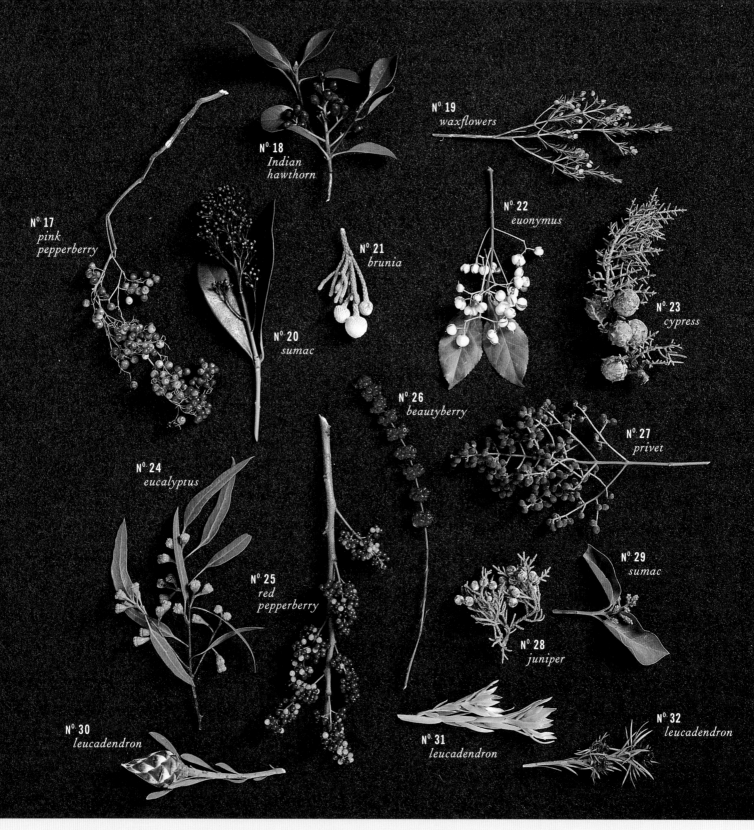

N⁰. 17
*pink
pepperberry*

N⁰. 18
*Indian
hawthorn*

N⁰. 19
waxflowers

N⁰. 20
sumac

N⁰. 21
brunia

N⁰. 22
euonymus

N⁰. 23
cypress

N⁰. 24
eucalyptus

N⁰. 25
*red
pepperberry*

N⁰. 26
beautyberry

N⁰. 27
privet

N⁰. 28
juniper

N⁰. 29
sumac

N⁰. 30
leucadendron

N⁰. 31
leucadendron

N⁰. 32
leucadendron

*bayberry (**13**), has aromatic silver-gray berries. Pittosporum (**14**) is common in southern gardens. Pyracantha, or firethorn (**15**), is a thorny shrub with glossy leaves and red, yellow, or orange fruit. The familiar juniper (**16, 28**) produces small, long-lasting, powdery-blue fruit. Schinus, or pepperberries (**17, 25**) are plentiful at florists' shops during the holiday season. The warm-climate shrub Rhaphiolepis indica, or Indian hawthorn (**18**), has blue-black berries and small glossy leaves. Unopened Chamaelaucium, or waxflowers (**19**), look like tiny berries. Rhus, or sumac (**20, 29**), is easy to grow. Brunia (**21**) has almost scaly foliage and long-lasting silver fruit. A variety of euonymus (**22**) are grown across the country. Many Cupressus, or cypress (**23**), trees produce dull-purple to silver fruit. Callicarpa, or beautyberry (**26**), shrubs are known for their shapely fruit. Many hardy varieties of Ligustrum, or privet (**27**), produce small, hard, dark-blue to purple fruit.*

FLOWERS AND BERRIES *Vivid red flowers and greenery never fail to evoke the spirit of the holidays.* LEFT: *Sprays of holly (*Ilex crenata *and* I. *'Autumn glow') frame a bouquet of roses and carnations.* BELOW: *Taper candles are ringed with spidery cream chrysanthemums, russet roses, and the glossy red berries of St. John's Wort.*

ROSE CANDLESTICKS

YOU WILL NEED *roses ∗ chrysanthemums ∗ fourteen-gauge floral wire ∗ taper candles ∗ candlesticks ∗ St. John's Wort berries*

Trim stems of flowers just below base—you'll need about four or five per candle-stick, depending on size. Thread flowers onto wire by piercing each one through base. Form a ring slightly larger than candle; tie wire to secure. Slide on candle-sticks; arrange berries between blooms. There is no need to wire berries in place.

MISTLETOE TABLE *Dangling over a doorway, mistletoe inspires kisses. With its delicate foliage and almost translucent berries, it is even lovelier in a lush display. Once brought indoors, the greenery will stay fresh for just a few days, so reserve it for a special event, like a holiday party. Here, a dainty mistletoe garland—overlapping bundles wired together by their stems—encircles a punch table.*

LIGHTED WREATH AND GARLAND

YOU WILL NEED *double-wire wreath form * wire cutters * two strands red pearl lights * 28-gauge floral wire * dried pepperberries * wired miniature glass balls * satin ribbon * evergreen garland*

Remove part of a double-wire wreath form with wire cutters to make a horseshoe shape. Weave pearl lights onto form, ending strands at top center. Carefully wire bundles of dried berries around lights, along with wired glass balls (available at craft or florists' shops). Tie wreath at top center with ribbon, disguising light cords, and string it over a door. The evergreen garland is also illuminated with pearl lights; bundles of pepperberries adorn the light fixtures.

WREATH AND GARLAND

YOU WILL NEED *twenty-eight-gauge floral wire on spool or paddle • double-wire wreath form • bundles of berries • rope*

Large bundles of berries, framed by their own greenery, make for casual, bountiful decorations. **1.** Handfuls of *Nandina domestica,* or heavenly bamboo, make a loose wreath. You can follow these basic instructions to make decorations with whatever berries are available. To make a wreath, secure the end of floral wire that is on a spool or paddle to a double-wire wreath form. Lay a bundle of berries on form, and wrap wire around stems; do not cut. Add another bundle so that berries overlap stems of the first. Continue adding and wrapping until form is covered, then cut and secure wire. **2.** To make a garland, cut a piece of rope or wire to desired garland length. For the red pepperberry garland at left, we tied a knot in the middle of the rope to help us give the illusion of the berries growing out from the center: Starting at one end, wire bundles of berries to the rope, overlapping each bundle slightly with the next, as in the wreath technique. For a fuller look, crisscross bundles as you go rather than lay them all in one direction. Continue adding bundles of berries until you reach the knot in the center, then start adding bundles at other end.

A PAIR OF HOLIDAY WREATHS ABOVE: *Neat clusters of ball-shaped* Berzelia *and spiky buds of* Pieris, *both in shades of pink and green, make a well-manicured wreath that is finished with wide moiré ribbon. The circular single-wire wreath form was stretched into an oval, a hard-to-find shape.* LEFT: *Silver ribbon echoes the metallic sheen of viburnum tinus berries, nestled among bundles of privet. The densely clustered berries allow for a fuller-than-usual wreath.* OPPOSITE: *Greenery and berries are silhouetted against gift papers in deep, wintry shades.*

WINTER-BERRY CARDS

YOU WILL NEED *greenery and berries ∗ spray mount ∗ uncoated card stock ∗ spray paint ∗ white glue ∗ fine and coarse glitter*

1. Prune and press sprigs of greenery flat between heavy books for a few days. Then apply spray mount, and place on uncoated card stock. Spray lightly with paint in a dark, complementary shade—we used black, brown, and red—covering whole card. Let dry; remove greenery. **2.** Dot on white glue with a fine-tipped applicator to make "berries." Sprinkle with a mixture of fine and coarse glitter; blow excess glitter off card, taking care not to inhale. Center finished card on top of the lid of a decorative box.

PINECONES

nature's ornaments

✳

This year, leave one box of glass ornaments in the attic. Make some room among the glittering tinsels and shimmering ribbons that usually define your holiday decorating. Now take a look at what your Christmas evergreens wear when they're outside—these naturally beautiful ornaments deserve to accompany a tree indoors.

Pinecones are the hallmarks of conifers—literally, cone-bearing trees; they produce and store the seeds of a tree, and, with their shape and construction—overlapping, woody scales—they almost resemble tiny trees themselves. Since childhood, we have been fascinated by these perfect structures. We find them littering the ground each autumn and wonder over their potential: Their original purpose accomplished, the empty vessels seem to be waiting patiently for us to gather them up and make them into something new.

There are countless ways to use pinecones to evoke the spirit of the holiday season. Some of the simplest include filling bowls with them for centerpieces; tossing them into the fireplace for pine-scented kindling; and slathering them with peanut butter and seeds, then hanging them outdoors for neighborhood birds. But they are also ideal for any number of more complex craft projects. On the following pages, we've provided instructions for making tree ornaments, wreaths and garlands, picture frames, even an entire winter village from pinecones and other simple, readily available materials. Give them a try. One project might just grow into a wonderful new holiday tradition.

SNOWY CONES *A silvery, snow-covered evergreen appears to have been cast under a magical winter spell: Pinecones in all shapes and sizes, lightly dusted with glitter, mingle with delicate pinecone angels. Garlands of tiny cones and colorful beads drape from bough to bough.*

PINECONE ORNAMENTS

. . . .

YOU WILL NEED *pinecones * sponge-brush * craft glue * fine glitter * wired gold or silver tinsel * hot-glue gun * wooden beads * gold twine * seed beads * miniature glass balls * strong sewing needle * heavy-duty thread * glass beads*

. . . .

Select a variety of pinecones in different shapes and sizes for an attractive display. Smooth spruce cones (we used red and white spruce) are best for angel bodies, and tiny tamarack cones work well for stringing on a garland. **1.** To glitter pinecones for any of these projects, hold a cone carefully, and brush craft glue over tips of scales. **2.** Then, holding cone over bowl, spoon fine glitter over scales. **3.** To make an angel, shape wings from a length of wired gold or silver tinsel: Form a figure-eight, twisting the wire around on itself to secure. Pinch ends together to create the wing shape, and hot-glue to the back of a glittered pinecone. With a shorter piece of wired tinsel, form a halo shape. Hot-glue the wooden bead head to the top of the cone (hole

facing up); then glue the halo, as well as a looped length of gold twine to serve as a hanger, into the hole on top of the head. Use tiny dabs of craft glue to attach seed beads to the face for eyes and nose. Attach two shorter lengths of tinsel to each side of the pinecone for arms, if desired. **4.** For drop ornaments, hot-glue miniature glass Christmas balls (you can unstring a garland of balls for this purpose) between three pinecones, arranged in descending size. You can snip off the end of each pinecone, if necessary, to make a flat place to glue a ball. Run twine through the hole in top ball for a hanger. **5.** For a garland, use a strong sewing needle and heavy-duty thread to string tiny pinecones, alternating with red and green glass beads, until desired length is reached.

PINECONE GLOSSARY

The tiniest pinecones come from the tamarack (1), black spruce (7), and the hemlock (9). The red pine (3) and the fast-growing Austrian pine (11) produce smallish, rounded cones. The largest cones come from the sugar pine (2), native to the northwestern United States. Ponderosa (4) is another northwestern tree. The slash pine (10) is a Florida native. The white pine (13) is a southern favorite. The Jack pine (12) likes a cool climate. The cones of the Norway and white spruces (6, 8) have dense, smooth scales. The longleaf pine (5) produces the largest cones in the eastern U.S.

Nº 1
tamarack

Nº 2
*sugar
pine*

Nº 3
*red
pine*

Nº 4
ponderosa

Nº 5
*longleaf
pine*

Nº 6
*Norway
spruce*

Nº 7
*black
spruce*

Nº 8
*white
spruce*

Nº 9
hemlock

Nº 10
*slash
pine*

Nº 11
*Austrian
pine*

Nº 12
*Jack
pine*

Nº 13
*white
pine*

PINE-FRAMED MEMORIES *Tiny picture frames made of pinecone scales become charming keepsake ornaments when filled with favorite photographs and suspended on ribbons. Glass ornaments continue the pinecone theme.* OPPOSITE: *A potted Christmas tree, festooned with pinecone garlands, glass ornaments, and framed photos demands a closer look; each ornament, like an entry in a living scrapbook, tells a story.*

PICTURE-FRAME ORNAMENTS

YOU WILL NEED *pinecones ∗ floral clippers ∗ template ∗ color photocopier ∗ photographs ∗ card stock ∗ hot-glue gun ∗ decorative paper ∗ craft glue ∗ ribbon*

You can use your favorite pinecones for this project. **1.** Remove scales with small floral clippers. **2.** Glue or color photocopy photograph onto card stock. Using a template for a circle or other shape (you can make it yourself or buy one ready-made at a craft store), outline a photograph or color photocopy with a pencil. Cut out. Hot-glue pinecone scales around perimeter of the back of the photograph, so the scales peek over the edge. Alternatively, you can glue scales onto the front of the cut-out photograph. Finish ornament with decorative paper glued to back with a few dots of craft glue; glue a looped length of ribbon between paper and photo to make a hanger.

PINECONE WREATH

YOU WILL NEED *hot-glue gun ∗ wooden picks ∗ pinecones ∗ floral wire ∗ floral tape ∗ brush and craft glue ∗ fine glitter ∗ double-wire wreath form ∗ ribbon*

A dense, elegant wreath of pinecones is a quintessential Christmas accessory. **1.** Use picked pinecones, as sold in some floral shops, or make your own: Hot-glue a wooden pick (available at craft stores) to base of each cone; cut it to one inch in length, wrap it in a longer piece of wire, and cover pick and wire with floral tape. Then glitter cones (see technique, page 102). **2.** One at a time, place cones on a double-wire wreath form, building an attractive shape on three sides (leave back flat for hanging). Attach a wide ribbon to back of wreath form; tie in a bow.

PINECONE ELVES

YOU WILL NEED *colored and metallic pipe cleaners * white and green chenille bump pipe cleaners * black seed beads * pinecones * wooden beads * white glue * hot-glue gun or craft glue * glitter (optional) * miniature wooden stump*

Constructing pinecone elves for a village scene (pages 108 and 109) is fun for kids on a winter afternoon—just be sure to use craft glue instead of hot glue for safety if young children are involved. If you use craft glue, a longer drying time will be required before figures are stable. Begin by gathering all materials. You can use whatever pinecones you have available; to reconstruct ours,

you'll need the following: Eastern Scotch pinecone for the body of the old elf; mugo pinecones for bodies of girl and boy elves; the top of an Eastern Mountain "Star" hemlock for the girl's hat and reindeer's head; a red spruce pinecone for the reindeer body; and scales of longleaf pinecone for reindeer legs. You'll also need an acorn top for the boy's hat. If you want glittered cones, see page 102. **1.** To make the old elf, begin by shaping pipe cleaners into arms and legs and cutting a strip of white chenille pipe cleaner for his beard. For eyes and mouth, attach tiny black seed beads to his wooden-bead head (holes facing sides) with white glue. Also use seed beads to make faces of other figures. **2.** To make the old elf's hat, spiral a red metallic pipe cleaner into a cone shape by wrapping it around your little finger. Attach hat and beard to the bead head by push-

ing them into the holes on the sides of the wooden bead. For boy, girl, and reindeer, attach hair, hats, and antlers to heads with hot glue. **3.** Arms and legs for the elves are simply pushed into the pinecone bodies to secure; the four legs of the reindeer should be hot-glued in place. For each of the characters, the heads should be hot-glued to the bodies. A small wooden stump will make a perfect seat for the old elf (you don't have to attach it to him); in his hand put an even tinier pinecone.

RUSTIC VILLAGE *In this quaint, illumi-nated village, birch twigs make doors and window frames for weathered bass-wood buildings. Rooftops are shingled with pinecone scales and pine needles. Moss and balsam sprigs cover the ground (and a string of small electric lights).* OPPOSITE: *A reindeer and a family of elves frolic on a snowy hillside with longleaf pine scales for sleds.*

PINECONE HOUSES

YOU WILL NEED *photocopier · 3/32-inch-thick basswood cut into six-by-twenty-four-inch pieces · utility knife · paintbrushes · wood glue · masking tape · sandpaper · mahogany or walnut stain · oil-based white enamel paint · pinecones · hot-glue gun · pine needles · thin birch twigs · parchment paper*

1. Photocopy the templates on page 137, enlarging to two hundred percent. Then photocopy the enlargements, increasing their size by one hundred and twenty-five percent. Lay each copy over a piece of 3/32-inch-thick basswood. For easier cutting, position wood so most cuts will be made with the grain. To mark the shape, use a pin to prick the corners of the house and the other points where the edges meet, including the windows. Using a ruler, connect points. **2.** Use a utility knife to cut out all pieces and windows. **3.** To erect walls, use a small brush to apply wood glue along edges of two adjoining walls. Stand them upright, abutting each other. Hold in place with masking tape. Erect third wall in the same manner, then the last. Measure placement of roof panels: Both eaves should hang equally over each side. The longer roof panel should slightly overlap the peak; the second panel should abut underside of the first panel when glued in place. Brush wood glue along edges. Hold in place with masking tape. Let glue dry one hour. Remove masking tape. Sand adjoining edges if needed. **4.** Use a dry brush to apply dark wood stain and white enamel paint to walls, mixing them together as you work. Let dry thirty minutes. Apply more coats if desired. Lightly sand paint for an authentic weather-beaten look. **5.** To make shingles, take a small pinecone by its base; with your hands, split apart down its core. Pull off scales. Using a hot-glue gun, dab glue on narrow end of scale on concave side. Starting at bottom edge of one roof panel, lay down shingles, side by side, slightly overhanging side edges and bottom edge of roof panel. Continue laying shingles in rows that slightly overlap. Repeat on second roof panel. For roof peak: Start at midpoint, and hot-glue a row of scales along peak, wider ends of scales facing outer edge of peak. Repeat on remaining half, with wider ends facing opposite outer edge. To create different roof styles, vary the pinecones or use pine needles. Find pine needles that are longer than roof panels. Dab glue on needle joints, and lay the needles on roof panel, joints at roof peak. You may need layers of needles to cover roof. Glue individual needles lengthwise along peak. Paint inner edges of windows with dark stain. **6.** To detail windows, use a utility knife to cut four lengths of thin birch twigs slightly longer than window measurements. Shave down twigs lengthwise with a utility knife to get a flat surface. Miter ends. To make window crossbars, measure inner width and length of window. Cut a thin twig to each of these dimensions. Use a utility knife to carve a groove in middle of each. Dab wood glue into one groove; place one twig over other one to form a T. Dab wood glue onto each end; place crossbars in window. Glue frame around window, piece by piece, flat side down. For each window, cut a piece of parchment paper slightly bigger than window. Glue against windows from inside house. **7.** Paint a door in a color slightly darker than house. To make door frame, cut two pieces of thin birch twig slightly longer than door height and one piece slightly longer than door width (the door is 1 by 1 3/4 inches). Shave down each twig lengthwise with utility knife to get a flat surface. Miter ends. One by one, glue in place, flat side down. Shave off a small bud or cut a small cross section from a branch for a doorknob, and glue in place on door.

CHURCH AND VILLAGE

YOU WILL NEED *materials for pine-cone houses • string of lights • moss and evergreen sprigs or artificial snow*

Construct steeple and church separately following steps one through five for the pinecone house; the peak shingles on the church, though, should run in only one direction. For window frames, follow step six. Each church window has two crossbars; the windows in the steeple have no crossbars, just frames. To make the door frame, you will need four twigs of birch: two glued standing straight up, two glued forming a peak. The door is two inches tall with one-inch-long peaks. Create a double-door effect by gluing a thinner twig down the center of the door, and create two doorknobs by gluing a tiny twig cross section on each side of the center twig. Arrange village on a tray with lips. To illuminate buildings, place one light beneath each building, and cover cord and ground with moss and sprigs of evergreen. You can also hide cords with artificial snow.

PINECONE DETAILS

YOU WILL NEED *pinecones* * *floral clippers* * *hot-glue gun* * *picture frames* * *gift boxes*

You can use pinecones to add a festive and personal touch to store-bought picture frames and other objects. **1.** These cones are, clockwise from left, "Pink" Eastern white pine, Eastern white pine, Scotch pine, and pine spruce. To make florets, first remove scales from pinecones, using small floral clippers. **2.** Arrange scales into flower patterns, and use hot glue to hold them together. Then hot-glue finished florets to frames and gift boxes, in whatever pattern you like. The scales of different pinecones produce very different effects. We used (top row, from left): red spruce and Eastern white pine; second row: Scotch pine and Eastern white pine; third row: Eastern hemlock and "Pink" Eastern white pine; fourth row: Eastern hemlock and pine spruce.

PINECONE ACCESSORIES *Black-and-white family photos, both old and new, are unified with pinecone details. Embellishment can be as simple as a single row of scales or as intricate as a profusion of delicate pinecone clusters. A single floret also gives a bit of elegance to a plain wooden jewelry box.*

CHRISTMAS
PAST

When my daughter was only a month old, we found our country house in a remote section of the Berkshire Mountains in Middlefield, Massachusetts. We had allotted a very small budget to the purchase of a weekend place, a refuge from New York City where I could garden, Andy could build, and Alexis, our only child, could grow and thrive in the pure mountain air. ✳ We bought a one-room schoolhouse on Clark Wright Road to which three small rooms had been added over the years. The house had no bathroom and no running water, only a rain barrel under the leader from the roof gutter and plenty of ice-cold mountain water from a stream about a quarter-mile away. We took turns, Andy and I, lugging water in large pails from the stream to cook with, wash up with, and drink. It was always a pleasure to be there in warm weather, but in winter the place took on a special charm. For Alexis's fourth Christmas, we decided to attempt a holiday with no relatives, no heat, and no frills. Perhaps this is why it remains, in both my and Alexis's memories, one of our happiest times together. ✳ We arrived in Middlefield three days before Christmas. When we got there, the house was bitterly cold. We lit fires in the fireplace, the potbellied stove, and the Glenwood cook range. We wrapped Alexis in down quilts, and she read her books next to the blazing stove. After a cozy dinner, we went to bed early with the sunset. ✳ The next day we went to the woods to cut down a tree. A fresh blanket of snow had fallen, and it was hard to walk. Little Bear, our silver keeshond, struggled, and Alexis kept falling and laughing, the snow in places deeper than she was tall. We found a perfect tree, a fir covered with its own small pinecones, sawed it down, and dragged it back to the cottage. We stood it in our living room and decorated it with homemade ornaments— cookies, paper chains, strings of cranberries, popcorn, and pinecones, and origami creations that Alexis and I made from colorful papers Andy had brought from Japan. While we worked, we listened to National Public

Radio from Amherst on our old console radio. They played music by Bach and Handel and broadcast readings from great writers like Dickens, O. Henry, and Hans Christian Andersen. We laughed and talked and finished the tree, thinking it was the most beautiful thing we had ever seen. It smelled so good and fresh; I remember it as if it were yesterday. ✳ Alexis was a very thoughtful child; buying gifts for her was not difficult. I searched the bookstores for books I had loved as a child, or ones that seemed perfect for that time. I read aloud to her a lot, so some of the books were

I've spent many Christmases with my daughter making simple, homemade gifts and ornaments. Here, pinecone-framed photos—one of Alexis posing with a goat, another of my mother on her wedding day—dangle from our family's tree.

ones that could be read aloud and understood then, and saved for perusal later when she could handle all the words herself. We opened our presents on Christmas Eve, after we had eaten a country dinner cooked entirely on the wood-burning range. We had roast duck, sweet potatoes, and apple tart. The pastry, the skin of the duck, the caramelized flesh of the potatoes—I remember it as if it were yesterday. ✳ On Christmas morning we strapped on our cross-country skis and followed Andy's freshly cut trail into the hollow. We skied all the way to Glendale Falls, then found our way home and ate a

big breakfast of pancakes, local maple syrup, and bacon. The Christmas ham was in the oven, and the plum pudding was steaming atop the stove. Our friends from the village arrived to have Christmas dinner with us. Their two children, Anna and Bo, played with Alexis, and they all exchanged presents and told each other stories of the woods and winter. After frolicking outside until they were almost frozen, the children wrapped themselves up in blankets and whispered by the fire. ✳ I remember it as if it were yesterday. ✳ *Martha Stewart*

THE RECIPES

CRANBERRIES

CHEWY CRANBERRY-ALMOND COOKIES

MAKES ABOUT 2 DOZEN

Though delicate both in appearance and flavor, these cookies travel well in a gift box.

- ½ cup dried cranberries
- 4 ounces (about 1¼ cups) sliced blanched almonds
- ¾ cup granulated sugar
- ¼ cup all-purpose flour
- 1 teaspoon whole anise seed, crushed
- 3 large egg whites
- ¼ teaspoon coarse salt
- 2 tablespoons confectioners' sugar

1. Preheat the oven to 350°F. Line two baking sheets with parchment paper, and set aside.

2. Finely chop ¼ cup cranberries; set aside in a small bowl. Reserve remaining ¼ cup whole cranberries.

3. In the bowl of a food processor, process 3 ounces almonds (about 1 cup) with ½ cup granulated sugar until the almonds are finely ground. Transfer the almond mixture to a medium bowl. Stir in the flour, chopped cranberries, and crushed anise seed.

4. In the bowl of an electric mixer fitted with the whisk attachment, whisk the egg whites, salt, and remaining ¼ cup granulated sugar to soft glossy peaks. Fold egg-white mixture into dry ingredients until just blended.

5. Spoon level tablespoons of the batter 2 inches apart on the prepared baking sheets. Using remaining 1 ounce almonds and reserved whole cranberries, arrange 3 sliced almonds and 3 cranberries on top of each cookie. Sift confectioners' sugar over the cookies.

6. Bake until the cookies are lightly browned around the edges, about 12 minutes. Cool slightly before removing from sheets with a spatula. Transfer to a wire rack, and let cool. Cookies will keep up to 1 week in an airtight container at room temperature.

PISTACHIO-CRANBERRY BISCOTTI

MAKES ABOUT 2 DOZEN

Biscotti make good gifts because they keep well and travel without crumbling.

- 1½ cups shelled whole green pistachios
- 1 cup dried cranberries
  Grated zest of 1 lemon
- 1 teaspoon baking powder
- 2½ cups all-purpose flour, plus more for dusting
- 1¼ cups sugar
- ⅛ teaspoon coarse salt
- 3 large whole eggs
- 2 large egg yolks
- 1 teaspoon pure vanilla extract

1. Preheat the oven to 350°F. Place the pistachios in a single layer on a rimmed baking sheet; toast until they are aromatic, about 8 minutes. Shake the pan halfway through baking to make sure the nuts toast evenly. Let cool.

2. Line a rimmed baking sheet with parchment paper. Finely chop half the pistachios, and leave the rest whole; set aside.

3. In a small bowl, stir together the chopped and whole pistachios, cranberries, and lemon zest until combined.

4. In the bowl of an electric mixer fitted with the paddle attachment, combine the baking powder, flour, sugar, and salt. In a medium bowl, beat together the eggs, yolks, and vanilla. Add the egg mixture to the dry ingredients; mix on medium low until a sticky dough is formed. Stir in the nut-and-fruit mixture.

5. Turn the dough out onto a well-floured board; knead slightly. Shape into two 9-by-3½-inch logs. Transfer to the prepared baking sheet. Bake at 350°F until golden brown, 25 to 30 minutes. Remove from the oven. Reduce the oven to 275°F. Let logs stand until cool enough to handle, about 10 minutes.

6. On a cutting board, slice the logs on a diagonal into ½-inch-thick pieces. Return pieces cut side down to the baking sheet. Bake until lightly toasted, about 20 minutes. Turn over; bake 20 minutes more, or until slightly dry. Cool on a wire rack. Store in an airtight container for up to 2 weeks.

CRANBERRY VINEGAR

MAKES 2 CUPS

Use this as a nonfat condiment on its own, or whisk oil into it for a vinaigrette.

 2 cups fresh or defrosted frozen cranberries
 ½ cup honey
 ½ cup white wine
 1 garlic clove
 1 cup red-wine vinegar
 ¾ cup cranberry juice
 ¼ teaspoon freshly ground pepper

1. Combine the cranberries, honey, wine, and garlic in a saucepan; cover, and bring to a boil. Reduce heat to medium low, and simmer, stirring occasionally, until the cranberries are soft, about 20 minutes.

2. Pass the cranberry mixture through a food mill on the finest setting, pressing down to extract as much purée as possible. Discard solids.

3. Stir vinegar, juice, and pepper into the cranberry purée. Transfer to an airtight storage container, refrigerate, and use within 1 week.

CRANBERRY GLAZED TURKEY WITH CRANBERRY-CORNBREAD STUFFING

SERVES 8 TO 10

Covering the turkey with the moistened cheesecloth while cooking enables it to cook evenly and protects the delicate breast meat. Cranberry glaze adds a beautiful, rich sheen to the turkey and a slightly tart flavor.

 1 16- to 18-pound fresh whole turkey
 1 pound (4 sticks) unsalted butter, plus 4 tablespoons, softened
 1 750-ml bottle dry white wine
    Coarse salt and freshly ground pepper
    Cranberry-Cornbread Stuffing (recipe follows)
 5 red onions (about 2 pounds), peeled and quartered
    Cranberry Glaze (page 120)
 1 cup dry red or white wine, or water
 2 cups Homemade Chicken Stock (page 119) or low-sodium canned chicken broth

1. Rinse the turkey inside and out with cool water, and dry with paper towels. Let stand for 1 hour at room temperature, to ensure that the bird cooks evenly.

2. Preheat the oven to 450°F with a rack on the lowest level. In a large saucepan, melt 3 sticks butter, and add the bottle of wine. Turn the heat off, leaving the mixture on top of the stove to keep warm. Fold a large piece of cheesecloth into quarters, forming a 17-inch, 4-layer square. Immerse the cheesecloth in the butter and wine; let soak.

3. Place the turkey, breast side up, on a work surface. If the turkey comes with a pop-up timer, remove it; an instant-read thermometer is a much more accurate indication of doneness. Fold the wing tips under the turkey. Sprinkle inside the turkey with salt and pepper.

4. Fill the main turkey cavity with 7 to 8 cups stuffing. Clean off any stuffing that falls onto the outside of the bird. Tie the legs together loosely with kitchen twine (a bow will be easier to untie later). Fold the neck flap under, and secure with toothpicks. Brush the turkey with the 4 tablespoons softened butter, and sprinkle with salt and pepper.

5. Lift the cheesecloth out of the liquid, and squeeze it slightly, leaving it very damp. Spread it evenly over the breast and stretch to cover the wings.

6. Arrange the onions in a heavy metal roasting pan. Place the turkey in the pan. Transfer to the oven. Cook for 30 minutes. Reduce the temperature to 350°F. Slide oven rack out. Using a pastry brush, brush a quarter of the butter-wine mixture over the cheesecloth and exposed parts of the turkey, and continue to cook for 2 hours more, basting every 30 minutes. When all the butter-wine mixture has been used, melt the remaining stick of butter. Baste the turkey with half of that butter, and cook for 30 minutes more.

7. Insert an instant-read thermometer into the thickest part of the thigh. Do not touch the bone. The breast temperature does not need to be checked. If thermometer registers 169°F or below, baste turkey with remaining half stick of melted butter, and roast until thermometer register 170°F, 15 to 30 minutes more. Be careful to watch the pan juices; if pan gets too full, spoon out juices, reserving them for gravy.

8. Once the thigh temperature reaches 170°F, carefully remove and discard the cheesecloth. Using a pastry brush, apply half the cranberry glaze to the turkey. Cook the turkey for 10 to 15 minutes more. Apply the remaining glaze to the turkey, and cook 10 minutes more to set the glaze.

9. The turkey is fully cooked when an instant-read thermometer registers 180°F when inserted into the thigh. The stuffing should register between 140°F and 160°F. Transfer the turkey and the onions to a carving board or serving platter. Remove kitchen twine, and let stand about 30 minutes before carving.

10. While the turkey cools, make the gravy: Pour all the pan juices into a glass measuring cup. Let stand until the fat rises to the surface, about 10 minutes; skim off the fat.

11. Meanwhile, place the roasting pan over medium-high heat. Add 1 cup wine or water to the pan. Stir, using a wooden spoon, to loosen any browned bits on the bottom of the pan while the liquid comes to a boil. Add the stock to the pan. Stir well, and return to a boil. Cook until the liquid has reduced by half, about 10 minutes. Add the defatted pan juices, and cook over medium-high heat 10 minutes more. You will have about 2½ cups of gravy. Season with salt and pepper; strain into a warm gravy boat, and serve with the turkey.

CRANBERRY-CORNBREAD STUFFING

SERVES 10 TO 12

Stuffing and dressing are actually the same dish, but stuffing is cooked inside the bird and dressing is cooked separately in its own dish in the oven, creating a delicious crusty surface. This recipe makes enough for both, so guests may have their favorite choice. The recipe may be halved if less is desired.

- 2 cups pecans
- 12 tablespoons (1½ sticks) unsalted butter, plus more for dish
- 3 large onions, cut into ¼-inch dice
- 6 celery stalks, strings removed, cut into ¼-inch dice
- ¼ cup fresh oregano leaves, chopped
- 1½ quarts Homemade Chicken Stock (recipe follows) or low-sodium canned chicken broth
  Skillet Cornbread (recipe follows), crumbled
- 1 loaf stale white bread, crusts on, cut into 1-inch cubes (10 heaping cups)
- 3 large eggs, lightly beaten
- 2 cups dried cranberries
- 1 cup coarsely chopped fresh flat-leaf parsley (1 large bunch)
- 1 tablespoon coarse salt
- 1 tablespoon freshly ground black pepper
- ½ teaspoon cayenne pepper

1. Preheat the oven to 350°F. Place the pecans in a single layer on a rimmed baking sheet; toast until they are golden and aromatic, 8 to 12 minutes. Shake the pan halfway through baking to make sure the nuts toast evenly. Once cool, roughly chop the pecans; set aside.

2. Raise the oven temperature to 375°F. Butter a 7-by-12-inch baking dish or a 5-quart heat-proof glass dish; set aside.

3. Melt the butter in a large skillet. Add the onions and celery, and cook over medium heat until the onions are translucent, about 8 minutes. Add the oregano, stir to combine, and cook 2 minutes. Add ½ cup stock, and stir well. Cook for about 5 minutes, until the liquid has reduced by half.

4. Transfer the onion mixture to a large mixing bowl. Add the cornbread, bread cubes, eggs, pecans, dried cranberries, parsley, salt, black pepper, cayenne, and remaining 1 quart plus 1½ cups stock; mix to combine. Use to stuff turkey.

5. Transfer the extra stuffing to the prepared baking dish, and mound. Bake for 45 minutes or until the top is golden and stuffing is heated through.

HOMEMADE CHICKEN STOCK

MAKES 5 QUARTS

When using stock for a specific recipe, begin making it at least twelve hours ahead of time, and refrigerate for eight hours so the fat has a chance to collect on top and can be removed.

- 2 leeks, white and pale-green parts, cut into thirds, well washed
- 1 teaspoon whole black peppercorns
- 6 sprigs fresh dill or 2 teaspoons dried
- 6 sprigs fresh flat-leaf parsley
- 2 dried bay leaves
- 2 carrots, cut into thirds
- 2 celery stalks, cut into thirds
- 1 four-pound chicken
- 1½ pounds chicken wings
- 1½ pounds chicken backs
- 2 forty-eight-ounce cans (3 quarts) low-sodium chicken broth, skimmed of fat
- 1½ quarts cold water, or more

1. Place the leeks, peppercorns, dill, parsley, bay leaves, carrots, celery, whole chicken, wings, and backs in a large stockpot. Add the chicken broth and water, cover, and bring to a boil. Reduce to a very gentle simmer, and cook, uncovered, about 45 minutes. The liquid should just bubble up to the surface. A skin will form on the surface; skim it off with a slotted spoon, and discard, repeating as needed. After about 45 minutes, remove the whole chicken from the pot, and set it aside until it is cool enough to handle.

2. Remove the meat from the chicken bones, set the meat aside, and return the bones to the pot. Transfer the meat to the refrigerator for another use; if you plan to use it in soup, shred the meat before refrigerating it.

3. Continue to simmer the stock mixture, on the lowest heat possible, for 3 hours, skimming foam from top as needed. The chicken bones will begin to disintegrate. Add water if at any time the surface level drops below the bones.

4. Fill a very large bowl or sink with ice and water; set aside. Strain the stock through a fine sieve or a cheesecloth-lined strainer into a very large bowl. Discard the solids. Transfer the bowl to the ice bath; let stock cool to room temperature.

5. Transfer the stock to airtight containers. The stock may be labeled at this point and refrigerated for 3 days or frozen for up to 4 months. If freezing, leave the fat layer intact; it seals the stock. If refrigerating, chill for at least 8 hours, and remove fat before using.

SKILLET CORNBREAD

MAKES 1 LARGE SKILLET

We created this cornbread recipe to yield enough to make stuffing for an eighteen-pound turkey with plenty left over for a bowl of dressing. The cornbread may be made a day before the stuffing.

- ¼ cup pure vegetable shortening
- 2 cups all-purpose flour
- 2 cups coarse yellow cornmeal
- 2 tablespoons sugar
- 1 tablespoon plus 1 teaspoon baking powder
- 1½ teaspoons coarse salt
- 2 cups milk
- 4 large eggs

1. Preheat the oven to 425°F with the rack in center. Place the shortening in a 9- to 10-inch cast-iron, or other heavy, ovenproof, skillet. Transfer to the oven.

2. In a medium bowl, whisk together the flour, cornmeal, sugar, baking powder, and salt. Set aside. In another medium bowl, whisk together the milk and eggs until frothy. Pour the milk-egg mixture into the dry ingredients. Mix just until ingredients are incorporated. Do not overmix; batter should be lumpy.

3. Carefully slide out oven rack. Pour the batter into the hot skillet; return to the oven. Cook until the top is golden brown and a cake tester inserted in the center comes out dry, about 25 minutes.

CRANBERRY GLAZE

MAKES 1 CUP

This glaze may be made up to two days ahead and kept, refrigerated, in an airtight container. It is delicious brushed over chicken, duck, or pork, as well as turkey.

- 1 tablespoon unsalted butter
- ½ shallot, finely chopped (about 2 teaspoons)
- 2 fresh sage leaves
- 1 teaspoon whole juniper berries
- 1½ cups fresh or defrosted frozen cranberries
- 1 cup pure maple syrup
- 1 cup apple cider, plus more if needed
- ¾ cup red currant jelly
- ¼ teaspoon coarse salt
  Pinch of freshly ground pepper

1. In a medium saucepan, heat the butter over medium heat. Add the shallot, and cook until translucent, stirring occasionally, about 2 minutes. Add the sage leaves and juniper berries, and cook, stirring, for 1 minute. Add the cranberries, maple syrup, apple cider, jelly, salt, and pepper. Raise the heat to medium high, and simmer until the cranberries are soft and the skins split, about 3 minutes.

2. Transfer the cranberry mixture to a food processor, and purée until smooth. Pass the purée through a fine sieve into a small saucepan.

3. Return the glaze to the stove, and simmer gently over medium heat until the glaze has thickened slightly and yields about 1 cup, about 10 minutes. If the glaze seems too thick, thin with a little apple cider. Keep warm until ready to use.

GREEN PEA PUREE

SERVES 8 TO 10

The purée may be made up to one hour ahead and kept warm, covered with aluminum foil, in a heat-proof bowl, or in the top of a double boiler, set over a pan of simmering water.

- 1 teaspoon coarse salt, plus more for water
- 3 pounds fresh or defrosted frozen peas
- 2 tablespoons unsalted butter
  Pinch of freshly grated nutmeg
- ¼ teaspoon freshly ground pepper

1. Cover and bring a large pot of water to a boil; add salt. Fill a large bowl with ice and water; set aside. Working in two batches, cook the peas in the boiling water for about 1 minute, until bright green and tender. Using a slotted spoon, immediately transfer the peas to the ice bath. Drain the peas in a large colander.

2. Use a food mill fitted with the finest disk to purée the peas into a medium bowl. Transfer the purée to a medium saucepan placed over medium heat. Add the butter, nutmeg, salt, and pepper, and cook, stirring, until warmed through.

CRANBERRY-ORANGE RELISH

MAKES 2 CUPS

This is an easy addition to the Christmas menu, since it doesn't require any cooking.

- ¼ cup pecans
- 2 cups fresh or defrosted frozen cranberries
- ¼ cup finely chopped red onion
- 1 large jalapeño pepper, seeds and ribs removed, finely chopped
- 2 tablespoons freshly squeezed lime juice
- 2 blood oranges or navel oranges, peeled and sectioned, juice reserved
- 2 teaspoons grated fresh ginger
- ½ cup sugar
- 2 celery stalks, strings removed, cut into ¼-inch dice

1. Preheat the oven to 350°F. Place the pecans in a single layer on a rimmed baking sheet; toast until they are golden and aromatic, 8 to 12 minutes. Shake the pan halfway through baking to make sure the nuts toast evenly. Break the pecans into pieces.

2. Place the cranberries in a food processor, and pulse to chop coarsely, about 5 pulses. Transfer to a medium bowl.

3. Add the onion, jalapeño, lime juice, orange sections and juice, ginger, sugar, and celery; mix gently. Refrigerate for at least 1 hour and up to 2 days. Just before serving, add the pecans, and toss to combine.

CRANBERRY SAUCE WITH COGNAC

MAKES 1¼ CUPS

This is a spicy variation on traditional cranberry sauce.

- 2 cups fresh or defrosted frozen cranberries
- 3 tablespoons cognac
- 1 cup packed light-brown sugar
- ¼ cup freshly squeezed orange juice
- 3 whole allspice
- 2 whole cloves
- 4 whole black peppercorns
- ½ teaspoon crushed red-pepper flakes
  Cinnamon stick (½-inch piece)

1. In a medium saucepan, combine the cranberries, cognac, brown sugar, and orange juice. Place the allspice, cloves, peppercorns, red-pepper flakes, and cinnamon stick in a double layer of cheesecloth; tie into a bundle with kitchen string, and add to the saucepan.

2. Bring the mixture to a boil. Reduce to a simmer, and cook, stirring often, until syrupy, 15 to 20 minutes. Remove spice bundle; transfer to a bowl, let cool, and refrigerate until needed.

CRANBERRY-, ORANGE-, AND PINEAPPLE-FLAVORED VODKAS

MAKES THREE 750-ML BOTTLES

Flavored vodkas make attractive holiday gifts. If the flavored vodkas are decanted into their gift bottles with fruit remaining, store them in the refrigerator or freezer, for up to four months.

- 3 750-ml bottles vodka
- 1 cup fresh or defrosted frozen cranberries
- 1 orange, such as navel or blood, peel on
- 1 large ripe pineapple, trimmed and peeled

1. Decant 2 bottles of vodka into two clean lidded glass 2-liter containers. Soak the bottles to remove paper labels. Let dry, and reserve for gift giving.

2. To make cranberry vodka: Rinse the cranberries. Place the cranberries in one container of vodka. Allow to cure in the refrigerator or a cool, dark place for at least 1 week and up to 3 weeks.

3. To make orange vodka: Cut the orange in half. Place on a work surface cut sides down, and halve again to create quarters. Slice each quarter into ¼-inch-thick wedges. Add the orange wedges to the second container of vodka. Allow to cure in the refrigerator or a cool, dark place for at least 1 week and up to 3 weeks.

4. To make pineapple vodka: Slice the pineapple into ½-inch-thick rings. Arrange the pineapple rings in a clean, wide-mouthed 3-liter glass container. Pour the vodka from the third bottle over the pineapple and into the container. Allow to cure in the refrigerator for at least 1 week and up to 2 weeks.

5. If gift giving, use a funnel to pour the cranberry and orange vodkas back into their original reserved bottles. Decant the pineapple vodka: Use tongs or a wooden spoon to remove and discard the pineapple rings. Pour the pineapple vodka through a funnel into the original bottle. Serve icy cold.

CRANBERRY-BUTTERMILK SORBET

MAKES 1 QUART

Buttermilk, which is naturally low in fat, makes this refreshing dessert taste creamy.

- 1½ cups sugar
- 1½ cups water
- 2 cups fresh or defrosted frozen cranberries
- 1½ cups nonfat buttermilk
- 1 tablespoon pure vanilla extract

1. Bring the sugar and water to a boil in a saucepan. Reduce the heat to medium, and cook, stirring often with a wooden spoon, until sugar dissolves, about 10 minutes.

2. Meanwhile, place the cranberries in the bowl of a food processor; process to a smooth purée, about 2 minutes, scraping down the sides of the bowl several times. Add the cranberries to the hot syrup, and stir well. Cook 10 minutes more.

3. Fill a large bowl with ice and water. Pour the cranberry syrup into a bowl set over the ice bath. When cooled, transfer to the refrigerator until chilled. Add the buttermilk and vanilla to the cranberry syrup; transfer to an ice-cream maker, and freeze according to manufacturer's instructions. Store, frozen, in an airtight container for up to 1 week.

CRANBERRY UPSIDE-DOWN CAKE

MAKES ONE 8-INCH CAKE; SERVES 10

- 12 tablespoons (1½ sticks) unsalted butter, room temperature, plus more for pan
- ¾ cup all-purpose flour, plus more for pan
- 2¾ cups fresh or defrosted frozen cranberries
- ½ cup plus 1 tablespoon pure maple syrup
- ½ teaspoon ground cinnamon
- 1 teaspoon baking powder
- ¼ teaspoon coarse salt
- ¼ cup plus 2 tablespoons yellow cornmeal, preferably coarse
- ¼ cup almond paste
- ¾ cup plus 2 tablespoons sugar
- 3 large eggs, separated
- ¼ teaspoon pure vanilla extract
- ¼ teaspoon pure almond extract
- ½ cup milk

1. Butter and flour a professional 8-by-2-inch-round cake pan; set aside. In a large skillet, heat 6 tablespoons butter over medium heat until it sizzles. Add cranberries; cook until shiny, 2 to 3 minutes.

2. Add the maple syrup and cinnamon. Cook, stirring frequently, until the cranberries soften but still hold their shape, about 5 minutes. Remove the cranberries with a slotted spoon, and transfer to a baking sheet to cool slightly. Set skillet with syrup aside.

3. Arrange the cranberries in the prepared pan. Return the skillet with the syrup to medium heat until the syrup boils, 3 to 4 minutes; do not overcook. Immediately pour the syrup over the cranberries, and let cool about 10 minutes.

4. Place rack in the center of the oven, and preheat to 350°F. In a medium bowl, sift together the flour, baking powder, and salt. Mix in the cornmeal with a fork.

5. Place the remaining 6 tablespoons butter in the bowl of an electric mixer fitted with the paddle attachment. Crumble in the almond paste, and beat on medium speed until well combined, about 30 seconds. Gradually add ¾ cup sugar, and beat until creamy. Add the egg yolks, and beat until well combined. Beat in the vanilla and almond extracts. Add the flour mixture alternately with the milk in two batches. Transfer batter to a medium bowl; set aside.

6. Clean the mixer bowl. Using the whisk attachment, beat the egg whites in the mixer bowl until foamy. Slowly add the remaining 2 tablespoons sugar; beat until soft peaks form. Whisk a third of the whites into batter, then fold in remaining whites.

7. Spread the batter over the cranberries, and bake for 45 minutes, or until a cake tester inserted in the center comes out clean. Let the cake cool in the pan for 2 hours before inverting it onto a serving plate. Cake is best eaten within 2 days.

ICE

SHRIMP COCKTAIL

SERVES 12

Arranging and serving the boiled shrimp on an ice platter keeps them chilled for a party.

- 5 dozen large shrimp, shells and tails intact
  Coarse salt, for the water
- 2 dried bay leaves
- 1 tablespoon whole black peppercorns
  Ginger-Cilantro Cocktail Sauce (recipe follows)

1. Fill a large stockpot three-quarters full with water. Cover, and bring to a boil over high heat. Fill a large bowl with ice and water; set aside. Rinse the shrimp in a colander; place in the sink to drain.

2. When the water comes to a full boil, generously add salt, the bay leaves, and peppercorns. Keep the heat on high, and carefully transfer all the shrimp to the stockpot. Cook, stirring often, until the shrimp turn opaque and pink and start to float to the surface, about 4 minutes. Strain the shrimp, and transfer them to the ice bath.

3. Carefully peel the shrimp, making sure to leave the tails and last shell section intact. To devein the shrimp, run a sharp paring knife down the back of the shrimp, cutting deeply enough to meet the thin black intestinal tract. Remove the thin black vein with the tip of the paring knife. Refrigerate the deveined shrimp until ready to serve, up to several hours. Serve with the cocktail sauce.

GINGER-CILANTRO COCKTAIL SAUCE

MAKES 1⅓ CUPS

The fresh ginger and cilantro give this sauce an Asian flavor. The sauce may be made up to three hours ahead.

- 2 twenty-eight-ounce cans plum tomatoes
- 1½ tablespoons cider vinegar
- ⅓ cup sugar
- ¼ teaspoon coarse salt
- ¼ teaspoon ground allspice
- ¼ teaspoon ground cloves
- ¼ teaspoon ground ginger
- ¼ teaspoon cayenne pepper
- ½ teaspoon freshly ground black pepper
  Pinch of dry mustard
- 2 tablespoons grated fresh ginger
- 1 tablespoon chopped fresh cilantro
- 1 teaspoon finely chopped jalapeño pepper
  Juice of 3 limes

1. Push tomatoes and their juice through a strainer or food mill into a medium bowl. Transfer to a large saucepan over medium heat, and add the vinegar, sugar, salt, allspice, cloves, ginger, cayenne, black pepper, and mustard. Simmer until consistency is a little thinner than that of store-bought ketchup, about 50 minutes. Remove from heat, and let cool.

2. Add the fresh ginger, cilantro, jalapeño, and lime juice, and chill for 1 hour. Adjust seasonings before serving.

NUTS

CORNISH GAME HENS WITH PECAN–WILD RICE STUFFING

SERVES 4

Packages of mixed long-grain brown and wild rice are available in most grocery stores.

- 2 tablespoons unsalted butter, plus 3 tablespoons room temperature
- 8 ounces thick-cut bacon, cut into ½-inch pieces
- 1 large leek, white and light-green parts only, halved lengthwise, sliced crosswise into ¼-inch half moons, well washed
- 4 carrots, cut into ½-inch dice
- 4 celery stalks, strings removed, cut into ½-inch pieces
- 1 pound assorted mushrooms, such as shiitake, cremini, and chanterelle, wiped clean, stems removed, cut into ¾-inch pieces
- 2 cups long-grain brown–wild rice combination or brown rice
- ¼ cup dry white wine
- 1 quart Homemade Chicken Stock (page 119) or low-sodium canned chicken broth
- 6 ounces (about 1½ cups) pecans, roughly chopped
- 2 tablespoons fresh thyme leaves or 1 tablespoon dried
- ½ cup finely chopped fresh flat-leaf parsley
  Coarse salt and freshly ground pepper
- 4 Cornish game hens (or frozen hens that have been thawed)

1. Heat 2 tablespoons butter in a large shallow saucepan over medium heat. Add the bacon, and cook until just browned and cooked through, about 5 minutes. Add the leek, carrots, and celery, and cook until softened, about 5 minutes. Add the mushrooms, and cook until the juices are released and most of the liquid has evaporated, about 5 minutes or more.

2. Add the rice, and stir to combine. Add the wine, and stir until most of the liquid has been absorbed, about 2 minutes. Add the stock, and bring to a simmer over high heat. Reduce the heat to low, cover, and simmer until the rice is cooked through and the liquid has been absorbed, about 30 minutes. Stir in the pecans, thyme, and parsley. Season with salt and pepper. Set stuffing aside to cool completely.

3. Preheat the oven to 425°F. Rinse the hens, and pat dry. Sprinkle the cavities and outer skin of the hens with salt and pepper. Brush the skin with the remaining 3 tablespoons softened butter.

4. Stuff each hen with the prepared stuffing. Tie the legs of the hens with kitchen twine, and arrange in a medium roasting pan. Transfer the remaining stuffing to a 9-by-13-inch baking dish, cover with foil, and set aside.

5. Bake the hens for 20 minutes; then begin basting every 10 minutes with pan juices. Add the baking dish with the dressing to the oven after the first 20 minutes. Continue baking until the hens are golden and the juices around the leg joints run clear, about 30 minutes more for a total cooking time for the hens of 50 minutes. Remove kitchen twine, and arrange on a serving platter with the hot pecan dressing.

ALMOND BRIOCHE TOASTS

MAKES 10 SLICES

Blanched or unblanched almonds can be used, but unblanched almonds will make the toasts slightly darker. Day-old brioche works well for this recipe.

- 10 tablespoons (1¼ sticks) unsalted butter, room temperature
- ⅔ cup granulated sugar
- 5 ounces (1½ cups) finely ground almonds
- 1 large egg
- 1 teaspoon pure almond extract
- 1 twelve-ounce loaf brioche, sliced into 10 pieces
- ⅓ cup sliced almonds
  Confectioners' sugar, for dusting

1. Preheat the oven to 350°F. In the bowl of an electric mixer fitted with the paddle attachment, beat the butter and granulated sugar until creamy. Scrape down the sides of the bowl. Add the almonds, egg, and almond extract; beat until well combined.

2. Spread 3 tablespoons of the mixture onto each brioche slice. Garnish with almond slices, and place on an ungreased baking sheet.

3. Bake until the tops are golden brown and the brioche is toasted on both sides, about 20 minutes. Remove from the oven; transfer to a wire rack to cool. Dust with confectioners' sugar. Serve warm or at room temperature.

THREE-NUT PASTA

SERVES 4

Look for peeled and roasted, vacuum-packed chestnuts at your grocery store.

- ¾ cup blanched hazelnuts
- ¼ cup pine nuts
- ¼ cup extra-virgin olive oil
- 1 tablespoon unsalted butter
- 4 medium shallots, minced
- 16 fresh large chestnuts, roasted, peeled, and cut into quarters
- ½ cup dry white wine
- 1½ cups Homemade Chicken Stock (page 119) or low-sodium canned chicken broth
- ½ cup heavy cream
- 1 tablespoon coarse salt, plus more for seasoning
- 1 pound dried pappardelle pasta
- 2 tablespoons fresh thyme leaves
- ¼ cup fresh flat-leaf parsley, coarsely chopped
  Freshly ground pepper

1. Preheat the oven to 350°F with two racks. Place the hazelnuts and pine nuts in a single layer on two separate rimmed baking sheets. Toast until golden and aromatic, and the hazelnut skins begin to split, about 10 minutes. Set the pine nuts aside to cool. Rub the warm hazelnuts vigorously with a clean kitchen towel to remove the skins. Return to the baking sheet; toast about 1 minute more. Once cool enough to handle, coarsely chop the hazelnuts.

2. Cover and bring a large pot of water to a boil. Meanwhile, in a large skillet, heat 2 tablespoons oil and the butter over low heat. Add the shallots and chestnuts; cook until the shallots are tender and translucent, about 7 minutes. Add the wine, stock, and cream; raise the heat to high, and cook until the liquid is reduced by one-third, about 4 minutes.

3. Add the salt and the remaining 2 tablespoons olive oil to the boiling water. Drop the pasta into the water; stir. Cook until al dente. Drain.

4. Reduce the heat of the cream mixture to medium low; stir in the hazelnuts, thyme, and 2 tablespoons parsley. Season with salt and pepper; cook for 2 minutes more. Add the pasta, toss, and remove from the heat. Divide the pasta among four plates; drizzle the sauce on top. Garnish with pine nuts and remaining parsley.

HAZELNUT BRITTLE

MAKES ONE 11-BY-17-INCH SHEET

You can make this caramel brittle with other nuts, such as slivered almonds or pistachios.

- Vegetable oil, for pan and knife
- 4 cups sugar
- ¼ teaspoon apple-cider vinegar
- 1 cup water
- 5½ cups whole blanched hazelnuts

1. Oil an 11-by-17-inch baking pan; set aside. Combine the sugar, vinegar, and water in a medium saucepan placed over medium heat. Cook, stirring often, until the sugar dissolves. Stop stirring. Let the mixture continue to cook and color, swirling the pan as needed to distribute heat evenly. Brush down the sides of the pan with a wet pastry brush to remove any sugar crystals if needed. When amber in color, 20 to 22 minutes total, stir in the hazelnuts.

2. Pour the hot mixture into the pan. Let set until firm but still soft enough to cut. Invert onto a cutting board, and unmold. Working quickly, use an oiled chef's knife to cut the sheet into six equal rectangles. Store the brittle in an airtight container for up to 1 week.

SPICED NUTS

MAKES 2½ CUPS

When the egg white has been properly beaten, no clear liquid will remain on the bottom of the bowl.

- 1 large egg white
- ¼ cup sugar
- 1 teaspoon coarse salt
- ½ teaspoon chile powder
- ¼ teaspoon ground allspice
- ½ teaspoon ground cumin
- 1¾ teaspoons cayenne pepper
- 2½ cups pecan halves or assorted nuts, such as cashews, walnuts, or almonds

1. Preheat the oven to 300°F. In a medium bowl, use a whisk to beat the egg white until soft and foamy. In a separate bowl, combine the sugar, salt, chile powder, allspice, cumin, and cayenne; whisk into egg white.

2. Stir in the pecans or assorted nuts until well coated; spread the mixture in a single layer onto an ungreased rimmed baking sheet.

3. Bake the pecans for 15 minutes, then remove from oven. Using a metal spatula, toss, stir, and separate the nuts. Reduce heat to 250°F, and return the nuts to the oven; bake until medium brown, about 10 minutes.

4. Remove from the oven; toss, and stir again. Transfer the baking pan to a wire rack to cool. Break up any nuts that stick together; store in an airtight container for up to 2 weeks.

CHOCOLATE MACADAMIA-NUT TART

MAKES ONE 11-INCH TART

This tart is best baked several hours in advance and left at room temperature.

- ½ cup all-purpose flour, plus more for surface
- ½ recipe Pâte Sucrée (recipe follows)
- 2 large eggs
- 1 cup sugar
- ½ tablespoon bourbon
- ¼ teaspoon coarse salt
- 12 tablespoons (1½ sticks) unsalted butter, melted and cooled to room temperature
- 6 ounces semisweet chocolate, chopped
- 10½ ounces (2½ cups) unsalted whole macadamia nuts

1. Preheat the oven to 400°F. On a lightly floured surface, roll the pâte sucrée into a 14-inch circle. Fit the pastry into an 11-inch tart pan; trim the dough evenly along the edge. Use the trimmings to patch any thin spots in the shell. Refrigerate 30 minutes.

2. Meanwhile, in a large bowl, whisk eggs, sugar, and bourbon until combined. Whisk in the flour and salt. Whisk in the butter. Stir in the chocolate. Pour into the chilled tart shell. Cover the top with nuts, pressing them halfway down into the filling.

3. Bake for 10 minutes. Reduce heat to 350°F, and continue baking until the crust and nuts are golden, about 35 minutes more. If tart crust begins to get too brown, place aluminum foil over the top for remainder of cooking time. Transfer to a wire rack, and let cool.

PATE SUCREE

MAKES TWO 11-INCH TART SHELLS

This pastry dough may be stored in the freezer for up to one month. Defrost by refrigerating overnight or letting stand at room temperature for one hour.

- 2½ cups all-purpose flour
- 3 tablespoons sugar
- 1 cup (2 sticks) cold unsalted butter, cut into pieces
- 2 large egg yolks
- ¼ cup ice water

1. Place the flour and sugar in the bowl of a food processor; pulse to combine. Add butter; pulse until mixture resembles coarse meal, 10 to 20 seconds.
2. Lightly beat the egg yolks; add the ice water. Add to the food processor while the machine is running; process until the dough holds together.
3. Divide the dough into two batches; turn out onto two separate pieces of plastic wrap. Flatten each into a circle, and wrap in plastic wrap; refrigerate for at least 1 hour.

PECAN BUTTER COOKIES WITH CHOCOLATE CHUNKS

MAKES 2 DOZEN

If you prefer a chewy cookie, bake for fifteen minutes. For cakier cookies, bake for the full twenty minutes.

- 11 ounces (about 2½ cups) pecan halves
- ¼ cup plus 2 tablespoons vegetable oil
- ¾ teaspoon coarse salt
- 1 cup (2 sticks) unsalted butter, room temperature
- 1 cup packed light-brown sugar
- 2 large eggs, well beaten
- 2 teaspoons pure vanilla extract
- 3½ cups all-purpose flour
- 2 teaspoons baking soda
- 10 ounces bittersweet chocolate, chopped into chunks

1. Set aside 3 ounces (about 48) pecan halves. Combine the remaining 8 ounces pecans, vegetable oil, and ½ teaspoon salt in the bowl of a food processor. Process until mixture is very smooth and creamy, scraping down the bowl if needed. Set pecan butter aside.

2. In the bowl of an electric mixer fitted with the paddle attachment, cream together the butter and sugar on medium-high speed until light and fluffy, about 2 minutes. Scrape down the sides with a rubber spatula. Add the eggs, a little at a time, beating to combine between each addition. Add the vanilla, and beat to combine. Add the pecan butter, and beat to combine, scraping sides as needed with a rubber spatula.
3. Sift together the flour, baking soda, and remaining ¼ teaspoon salt. Reduce the speed of the mixer to low, and add the flour mixture in several additions. Use a rubber spatula to scrape sides as needed. Stir in the chocolate chunks. Wrap the dough in plastic, and chill at least 1 hour.
4. Preheat the oven to 350°F. Line two baking sheets with parchment paper; set aside. If you only have one baking sheet, keep half the dough in the refrigerator until the first batch is out of the oven.
5. Form the dough into twenty-four 1½-inch balls. Press two pecan halves into each ball, and place the balls about 2 inches apart on the prepared baking sheets. Bake until the cookies are golden around the edges and just set, 15 to 20 minutes. Remove from the oven; let stand several minutes before removing from the baking sheets.

ELIZABETH WEBB'S PECAN CHEWIES

MAKES ABOUT FORTY 1-INCH SQUARES

- Unsalted butter, softened, for pan
- 1 cup all-purpose flour, plus more for pan
- 4 large eggs
- 1 pound (2¼ cups) packed light-brown sugar
- 1 teaspoon coarse salt
- 1 teaspoon pure vanilla extract
- 6 ounces (about 1½ cups) pecan halves

1. Preheat the oven to 325°F. Brush a 9-by-13-inch baking pan with butter, and dust with flour, tapping out excess. Set aside.
2. In the bowl of an electric mixer fitted with the paddle attachment, beat the eggs. Add the sugar; beat to combine. Add the flour, salt, and vanilla; beat to combine.

3. Spread the pecans in the prepared baking pan in a single layer. Pour batter over the pecans.
4. Bake until the mixture is set, and a shiny crust has formed, about 35 minutes. Remove from the oven; let cool to room temperature before cutting into 1-inch squares. For the neatest squares, clean knife frequently. Remove squares from the pan with a narrow spatula.

YUMMY PECAN SHORTBREAD COOKIES

MAKES 1½ DOZEN

Chill the dough before forming the cookies.

- 14 tablespoons (1¾ sticks) unsalted butter, room temperature
- ½ cup confectioners' sugar, plus more for dusting
- 1 teaspoon pure vanilla extract
- 1 tablespoon ice water
- 2 cups all-purpose flour
- ¼ teaspoon coarse salt
- 8 ounces (about 2 cups) coarsely chopped pecans

1. Line a baking sheet with parchment paper, and set aside. In the bowl of an electric mixer fitted with the paddle attachment, blend the butter and sugar until soft and creamy. Add the vanilla and ice water; beat to combine.
2. In a separate small bowl, whisk together the flour and salt; with mixer on low, add to butter mixture, and stir to combine. Stir in pecans. Wrap dough in plastic; chill at least 1 hour.
3. Preheat the oven to 325°F. Form dough into about 1½-inch balls; arrange several inches apart on the prepared baking sheet. Using your fingers or the palms of your hands, press balls to flatten. Bake until bottoms of cookies are slightly brown, 20 to 25 minutes. Once cool, dust the cookies with confectioners' sugar.

PISTACHIO CHARLOTTE

MAKES ONE 8½-INCH CHARLOTTE

Store-bought ladyfingers can be used for forming the sides of the charlotte and cake layers. To make a cake round, place ladyfingers with one end of each facing center of pan, forming a circle shape.

¼ cup sugar
½ cup water
1 tablespoon kirsch
  Ladyfingers and Cake Rounds (recipe follows), ends of ladyfingers trimmed flat
  Pistachio Bavarian Cream and Praline (recipe follows)

1. Combine the sugar and water in a small saucepan; allow to simmer over low heat, stirring occasionally, until the sugar has dissolved, 1 to 2 minutes. Remove from heat, and allow to cool. Add the kirsch, and stir to combine.

2. Brush ladyfingers and cake rounds with syrup. Place the ladyfingers around the edge of an 8½-inch springform pan. Lay a cake round in the bottom, trimming, if necessary, to fit.

3. Spoon in one-third of pistachio bavarian cream, smooth the top, and sprinkle with one-third of pistachio praline. Repeat with the remaining cake rounds, bavarian cream, and praline to form two more layers. Place in the refrigerator to set, 4 to 5 hours, or overnight. Serve.

LADYFINGERS AND CAKE ROUNDS

MAKES ABOUT 22 LADYFINGERS
PLUS THREE 8½-INCH CAKE ROUNDS

Pipe the ladyfingers a half inch thick only, as they puff significantly while baking.

6 large eggs, separated
¾ cup granulated sugar
1¼ cups all-purpose flour
  Confectioners' sugar, for sprinkling

1. Draw three 8½-inch circles and four rows 3½ inches wide on parchment paper; place on baking sheets, and set aside. Prepare a large pastry bag with a ½-inch tip, and set aside.

2. Preheat the oven to 350°F with two racks centered. In the bowl of an electric mixer fitted with the whisk attachment, whisk the egg yolks and 11 tablespoons granulated sugar on high speed until the mixture is thick and pale, 1 to 2 minutes. Transfer mixture to a large bowl. Gently fold in the flour; set aside.

3. In the clean bowl of the electric mixer, fitted with the clean whisk attachment, beat the egg whites on low speed until frothy. While beating on medium-high, gradually add the remaining tablespoon granulated sugar; beat until stiff, 1 to 2 minutes. Fold one-third of the whites into the reserved yolk mixture to lighten, then fold in the remaining whites until just incorporated.

4. Using an offset spatula, spread batter evenly inside the circle guides, making circles ¼ inch thick. Bake in the oven, rotating sheets once, until light golden, about 15 minutes. Transfer to wire racks to cool.

5. While the cake rounds are baking, fill the pastry bag with the remaining batter, and pipe ladyfingers, ½ inch thick, between the lines drawn on the parchment paper.

6. Sprinkle the ladyfingers generously with confectioners' sugar, and allow the sugar to soak in, about 3 minutes. Transfer to the oven; bake, rotating sheets once, until light golden, 15 to 18 minutes. Transfer to wire racks to cool. Once the cake rounds and ladyfingers are cool, remove from parchment paper.

PISTACHIO BAVARIAN CREAM AND PRALINE

MAKES ABOUT 4½ CUPS CREAM
AND 2 CUPS PRALINE

Whole blanched almonds may be substituted for the pistachio nuts.

5½ cups whole pistachio nuts, shelled
3 cups milk
1¾ cups sugar
¼ cup plus 6 tablespoons water
1 tablespoon plus 1½ teaspoons unflavored gelatin
6 large egg yolks
1½ tablespoons kirsch
1¼ cups heavy cream

1. Preheat the oven to 325°F. Bring a medium pot of water to a boil over high heat. Add the pistachio nuts, and blanch for 30 seconds; drain. When nuts are cool enough to handle, remove the skins.

2. Place the nuts in a single layer on a rimmed baking sheet; toast until they are dry but still green, 10 to 20 minutes. Remove from the oven, and allow to cool. Set aside 1¼ cups nuts.

3. Transfer the remaining nuts to a food processor, and process until coarsely ground. Place ground nuts and milk in a medium saucepan, and bring to a boil over medium heat. Remove from heat, transfer to a medium bowl, and place in the refrigerator for 3 hours.

4. Make the praline: Line a rimmed baking sheet with a Silpat baking mat (see The Guide) or parchment paper; set aside. Place ¾ cup sugar and ¼ cup water in a small saucepan set over medium heat. Cook, stirring occasionally, and brushing down the sides of the pan with water as needed, until the sugar is golden, about 10 minutes.

5. Add the reserved 1¼ cups nuts, and stir to combine. Pour mixture onto the prepared baking sheet; allow to cool. Break into pieces, and place in the bowl of a food processor. Pulse until the caramel is coarsely chopped; set aside.

6. Sprinkle the gelatin evenly over 6 tablespoons of water in a small bowl. Set aside to soften.

7. Make the bavarian cream: Fill a bowl with ice and water; set aside. Remove the milk-nut mixture from the refrigerator, and strain through cheesecloth into a medium saucepan, squeezing all milk from the nuts. Discard nuts. There should be 2 cups strained milk. Bring the milk to a simmer over medium-low heat. While the milk is heating, whisk the egg yolks with the remaining cup sugar in a medium bowl, until pale and combined. Pour hot milk slowly into the egg mixture, whisking constantly. Return the egg-milk mixture to the saucepan, and cook, stirring constantly until it thickens and coats a spoon, 3 to 5 minutes. Do not let the mixture boil. Remove from heat, and stir in softened gelatin until completely dissolved. Strain the mixture into a clean bowl, and set over ice bath, stirring occasionally until the mixture is cold. Add the kirsch, and stir to combine.

8. Using an electric mixer fitted with the whisk attachment, beat the heavy cream to soft peaks. Fold whipped cream into the egg-milk mixture until just combined. Use immediately.

FRUITCAKE

BACKHOUSE FAMILY FRUITCAKE

MAKES ONE 8-INCH CAKE

- 12 tablespoons (1½ sticks) unsalted butter, room temperature, plus more for pan
- 4 ounces (½ cup) glacéed or dried pineapple, chopped into ½-inch pieces
- 4 ounces (½ cup) glacéed or dried apricots, chopped into ½-inch pieces
- 8 ounces (1½ cups) dates, pitted, chopped
- 4 ounces (½ cup) dried cherries (see The Guide)
- 4 ounces (¾ cup) whole blanched almonds
- 8 ounces (1½ cups) whole Brazil nuts
- ⅔ cup all-purpose flour
- ½ cup cake flour (not self-rising)
- ½ teaspoon baking powder
  Pinch of coarse salt
- 1 cup packed light-brown sugar
- 3 large eggs
- 1 teaspoon pure vanilla extract
- 2 tablespoons rum, plus more for dousing

1. Preheat the oven to 300°F. Brush an 8-inch springform pan with soft butter. Line bottom and sides with parchment; brush with butter.
2. Combine the pineapple, apricots, dates, cherries, almonds, and Brazil nuts in a bowl; set aside. In another bowl, sift both flours, baking powder, and salt.
3. In the bowl of an electric mixer fitted with the paddle attachment, beat the butter and sugar on medium-high speed until fluffy, about 3 minutes. Reduce the speed; add the eggs, one at a time, mixing well after each addition. Add the vanilla and rum.
4. In two additions, add the dry ingredients to the butter. Scrape down the bowl between additions. Fold in the fruit and nuts. Pour batter into the pan. Bake until golden and set, about 2½ hours. Cover with foil if it colors too much.
5. Transfer to a wire rack, and let cool. Remove from the pan; discard the parchment. Wrap in cheesecloth or muslin. Douse with ¼ cup rum. Wrap in plastic or keep in an airtight container. Store in a cool, dark, dry place; douse with ¼ cup rum weekly for at least 1 month before serving.

FRUIT AND STOUT CAKE

MAKES ONE 9-INCH LOAF

- 1 cup (2 sticks) unsalted butter, room temperature, plus more for pan
- 12 ounces (2 cups) prunes, pitted, chopped into ½-inch pieces
- 8 ounces (1½ cups) golden raisins
- 8 ounces (1½ cups) currants (see The Guide)
- 1¼ cups stout, such as Guinness, plus more for dousing
- 2⅔ cups all-purpose flour
- ½ teaspoon baking powder
- ¼ teaspoon freshly grated nutmeg
- ¼ teaspoon ground cinnamon
- 1¼ cups packed light-brown sugar
- 2 large eggs

1. Preheat the oven to 300°F. Brush a 9-by-4½-inch loaf pan with butter. Line the pan with parchment; brush with butter. Set aside.
2. Combine the prunes, raisins, and currants in a medium bowl. Add ½ cup stout, and let stand.
3. In a medium bowl, sift the flour, baking powder, nutmeg, and cinnamon. In the bowl of an electric mixer fitted with the paddle attachment, cream the butter and sugar until fluffy, about 3 minutes. On medium speed, add the eggs, one at a time, mixing well after each, scraping down the sides twice. Add dry ingredients in two additions; mix just to combine. Fold in the fruit mixture.
4. Pour the batter into the prepared pan. Bake until dark brown and set, and a cake tester inserted into the middle of the cake comes out clean, about 3½ hours. (Cracks will appear on top of the cake.) Remove from the oven; douse with ½ cup stout. Let stand on a wire rack for 30 minutes. Remove from the pan, and discard parchment; let cake cool completely.
5. Wrap the fruitcake in cheesecloth or muslin. Douse the fruitcake with the remaining ¼ cup stout. Wrap in plastic or keep in an airtight container. Store in a cool, dark, dry place; douse with ¼ cup stout once a week for at least 1 month before serving.

CHOCOLATE PANFORTE

MAKES ONE 9-INCH CAKE

Unlike most fruitcakes, this one is ready to eat as soon as it cools.

- 4 ounces (¾ cup) whole hazelnuts
  Unsalted butter, softened, for pan
- 3 ounces (½ cup) dried cherries (see The Guide)
- 2 tablespoons brandy
- 3 ounces (¾ cup) best-quality unsweetened chocolate, finely chopped
- 1¼ ounces (¼ cup) best-quality bittersweet chocolate, finely chopped
- 1 cup plus ½ tablespoon all-purpose flour
- 1½ teaspoons ground cinnamon
- ⅔ cup honey
- ⅔ cup packed light-brown sugar
- ½ teaspoon best-quality cocoa powder

1. Preheat the oven to 350°F. Place the hazelnuts in a single layer on a rimmed baking sheet; toast until the skins begin to split, about 10 minutes. Rub the warm nuts vigorously with a clean kitchen towel to remove skins. Return to the baking sheet; toast until fragrant and golden brown, about 1 minute more. Let cool.
2. Reduce heat to 300°F. Brush a 9-inch springform pan with butter; fit with a circle of parchment. Brush parchment with butter; set aside.
3. Combine the cherries, nuts, brandy, and chocolates in a medium bowl; set aside. Sift 1 cup flour and ½ teaspoon cinnamon in a bowl.
4. Combine the honey and sugar in a saucepan. Stirring, bring the sugar mixture to a boil; reduce heat. Simmer for 2 minutes. Combine with cherry mixture, stirring until combined. Fold in the flour mixture; mix to combine. Pour into the prepared pan.
5. With wet hands or a small metal spatula, press the mixture to form a level layer. Combine the remaining ½ tablespoon flour, 1 teaspoon cinnamon, and cocoa. Sift over unbaked cake. Bake until set, about 30 minutes. Remove from the oven, and let cool. Gently brush off the flour coating before serving. Store in an airtight container for up to 1 week.

DOWAGER DUCHESS FRUITCAKE

MAKES FIVE 5¾-BY-3-INCH TEA LOAVES,
OR TWO 9-BY-5-BY-2½-INCH LOAVES

*This cake is best sliced as thinly as possible.
You may substitute store-bought candied
citrus peel (see The Guide).*

1 pound (4 sticks) unsalted butter, room
  temperature, plus more for pans
2 pounds plus 4 ounces (6 cups) Candied
  Citrus Peel, such as grapefruit, orange,
  or lemon, cut into ½-inch pieces (page 130)
15 ounces (2½ cups) whole almonds, blanched
2½ cups sugar
5 large eggs
3 tablespoons dry sherry, plus more
  for dousing
  Grated zest of 1 lemon
  Grated zest of 1 orange
4 cups all-purpose flour, sifted

1. Preheat the oven to 300°F. Brush pans with
butter. Line the bottom of pans with parchment, and brush with butter. Combine candied
citrus and almonds in a mixing bowl; set aside.

2. In the bowl of an electric mixer fitted with
the paddle attachment, cream together the butter and sugar until light and fluffy, about 3
minutes. Add the eggs, one at a time, beating
well after each addition and scraping down
the sides of the bowl at least twice. Stir in the 3
tablespoons sherry and citrus zests.

3. Reduce speed of the mixer to low. Add flour, 1
cup at a time, beating until just combined.
Fold in the candied citrus and almonds.

4. Pour the batter into the prepared pans. Bake
until golden and set, and a cake tester inserted
into the middle of each cake comes out clean,
about 1 hour 15 minutes for small cakes and 1
hour 45 minutes for large cakes.

5. Remove the cakes from the oven, and douse
with 3 tablespoons sherry. Transfer to a wire
rack, and let cool completely. Remove the cakes
from the loaf pans, and discard the parchment
paper. Wrap the cakes in muslin or cheesecloth.
Wrap in plastic or keep in an airtight container.
Store in a cool, dark, dry place, dousing cakes
with several tablespoons of sherry once a week
for at least 1 month before serving.

FIGGY CHRISTMAS FRUIT ROLL

MAKES FOUR 12-INCH ROLLS

*You may substitute store-bought candied
citrus peel (see The Guide).*

12 ounces (3¼ cups) walnut halves
4½ pounds (about 10 cups) dried figs
4 ounces (¾ cup) dates, pitted and
  roughly chopped
6 ounces (1 cup) Candied Citrus Peel, such
  as orange, roughly chopped (page 130)
7 ounces bittersweet chocolate, chopped
  into ¼-inch pieces
5 ounces (1 cup) pistachios
¼ cup plus 2 tablespoons brandy,
  plus more for dousing
2 tablespoons whole anise seed
1 teaspoon ground cinnamon
¼ teaspoon freshly ground nutmeg
1 teaspoon pure vanilla extract
  Pinch of coarse salt
  Confectioners' sugar

1. Preheat the oven to 350°F. Place the walnuts
in a single layer on a rimmed baking sheet;
toast until they are golden and aromatic, 8 to
12 minutes. Shake the pan halfway through
baking to make sure the nuts toast evenly. Let
the walnuts cool completely. Roughly chop
the walnuts.

2. Place the figs in the bowl of a food processor, and process until finely minced (you may
need to work in two batches). Transfer the
figs to a large bowl, and add the chopped walnuts. Add the dates, citrus peel, chocolate,
pistachios, 2 tablespoons brandy, anise seed,
cinnamon, nutmeg, vanilla, and salt; mix well,
using your hands for best results.

3. Divide the mixture into four equal parts. Dust
a clean work surface with confectioners' sugar. Gently roll each part into a log about 2 inches
in diameter and 12 inches long. Gently brush
off excess sugar with a pastry brush. Roll each
log in rice paper (see The Guide). Brush each log
with about 1 tablespoon brandy. Do not worry
if rice paper tears. Wrap logs again in parchment,
and secure with string. Wrap in plastic or keep
in an airtight container. Store in a cool, dark, dry
place, dousing rice paper with brandy once a
week for at least 1 month before serving. Slice
rolls into thin rounds to serve.

MR. AND MRS. MAUS'S FRUITCAKE

MAKES TWO 9-INCH CAKES OR LOAVES

1 pound (4 sticks) unsalted butter, room
  temperature, plus more for pans
2½ cups all-purpose flour, plus more for pans
2 tablespoons allspice
2 cups sugar
12 large eggs
6 pounds candied fruits and fresh nuts, such
  as citron, apricots, walnuts, and pecans
½ cup molasses
1 cup apricot jam
⅓ cup brandy
  Whole dried apricots
  Pecan halves

1. Preheat the oven to 275°F. Brush pans with
butter. Line with parchment paper; brush with
butter, and dust with flour, tapping out excess.
Set aside. In another bowl, sift together the flour
and allspice; set aside.

2. In the bowl of an electric mixer fitted with
the paddle attachment, cream the butter and
sugar until light and fluffy, about 3 minutes.
Add the eggs, one at a time, beating well after
each addition and scraping down the sides
of the bowl at least twice. Stir in the fruits, nuts,
and molasses; blend well.

3. Add the flour mixture to the batter, 1 cup at
a time, until well mixed.

4. Spoon the batter into the prepared pans. Set
the pans in a shallow pan filled with 1½ to 2
inches of hot water. Bake until set, and a cake
tester inserted into the middle of each cake
comes out clean, 3 to 3½ hours. Transfer the
pans to a wire rack to cool completely.

5. Remove the cakes from the pans; discard
the parchment paper. Strain the apricot jam;
place in a small saucepan. Add the brandy to
the pan, and heat over low heat until the mixture is warm through and syrupy. Glaze the
fruitcake with the mixture. Garnish with dried
apricots and pecan halves; glaze again. Let
the glaze harden before wrapping the fruitcake
in parchment paper. Wrap in plastic or keep
in an airtight container; store in a cool, dark,
dry place for several weeks.

PLANTER'S PUNCH

SERVES ABOUT 24

Serve this punch icy cold. In lieu of ice, you can freeze whole citrus in the freezer, and add it to the punch just before serving. The frozen fruit won't dilute the punch.

⅔ cup freshly squeezed lemon juice (4 lemons)
¾ cup freshly squeezed lime juice (5 limes)
1⅓ cups freshly squeezed orange juice
    (4 to 5 oranges)
1½ cups dark rum
1 forty-six-ounce can (6 cups) pineapple juice
½ cup sugar
¼ teaspoon bitters
1 liter sparkling water or club soda

Combine the lemon, lime, and orange juices in a large container. Add the rum, pineapple juice, sugar, and bitters, and stir to combine. Transfer the mixture to the refrigerator, and chill. Just before serving, stir in cold sparkling water or club soda.

ICED SPICE TEA

SERVES ABOUT 12

The frozen clove-spiked lemons act as ice cubes for this nonalcoholic punch.

6 lemons
  Whole cloves, for lemons
6 cranberry-flavored tea bags
6 cinnamon sticks
¼ cup star anise
2 tablespoons ground allspice
1½ quarts water

1. Pierce the skin of a lemon with a wooden skewer, creating a decorative design; fill each hole with a single clove. Repeat with the remaining lemons. Transfer the studded lemons to the freezer, and let freeze at least several hours; overnight is best.
2. Combine the tea, cinnamon sticks, star anise, allspice, and water in a medium saucepan. Cover, and bring to a simmer over medium heat. Uncover, letting the mixture simmer for the flavors to combine, about 15 minutes. Cool to room temperature. Transfer to an airtight container, and refrigerate until cold. The spice tea may be made up to a day ahead.
3. To serve, strain the cold tea into a punch bowl. Add the frozen lemons to keep the punch cold.

STAR ANISE GRAVLAX

MAKES ABOUT 4 DOZEN

Gravlax is a good food to serve at parties because it must be made ahead.

2 tablespoons sugar
3 tablespoons coarse salt
4 whole star anise
12 whole black peppercorns
2 pounds fresh salmon fillet, skin on,
   bones removed
2 cups fennel fronds, chopped,
   plus more whole for garnish
1 lemon, thinly sliced
2 tablespoons vodka
  Sesame Star Crackers (recipe follows)
½ small bulb fennel, sliced paper thin
1 small red onion, sliced paper thin

1. Combine the sugar, salt, star anise, and peppercorns in a spice grinder or mortar and pestle, and grind until the spices are well crushed. Rub both sides of the salmon well with the mixture.
2. Arrange the chopped fennel fronds, lemon slices, and any leftover seasoning mixture in a glass baking pan large enough to hold the fish flat. Sprinkle the flesh side of the fish with vodka, and place in the dish, skin side up.
3. Cover the fish with plastic wrap, and place a wooden cutting board on top. Weight with cans. Cure in the refrigerator for 2 to 3 days. The salmon should look opaque when done.
4. Remove the fish from the baking dish, and brush off the seasonings. Serve immediately, or rewrap and refrigerate for 1 to 2 days.
5. To serve, slice very thinly on an angle down to the skin, using a very sharp slicing knife. To assemble hors d'oeuvres, top each cracker with a slice of gravlax, fennel, and red onion, and a sprig of fennel frond. Serve immediately.

SESAME STAR CRACKERS

MAKES ABOUT 4 DOZEN

Use a one-and-a-half-inch star-shaped cookie cutter to make bite-size crackers.

¼ cup plus 2 tablespoons black sesame seeds,
   toasted (see The Guide)
2 cups all-purpose flour, plus more for board
¾ teaspoon coarse salt
¼ cup plus 1 tablespoon dark sesame oil
½ cup water

1. Preheat the oven to 325°F. In a medium bowl, combine the sesame seeds, flour, and salt. Stir in the sesame oil with a fork until fine crumbs form. Add the water, and stir until the dough comes together.
2. Turn dough out onto a lightly floured board, and knead a few times until smooth. Wrap in plastic wrap, and let rest for 10 minutes.
3. Divide the dough into four equal pieces, and roll out to ⅛ inch thick. Cut into stars using a star-shaped cookie cutter. Prick each star with a fork in several places, and place on an ungreased baking sheet at least 1 inch apart.
4. Bake until just brown, 20 to 25 minutes. Transfer to wire racks, and let cool. Store the crackers in an airtight container, at room temperature, until ready to use. Crackers will keep up to 1 week.

ROASTED LOIN OF PORK WITH ORANGE, FIG, AND PRUNE STUFFING

SERVES 6

The pork marinates overnight in the refrigerator, so plan ahead. Use a heavy roasting pan if you don't have a skillet large enough to hold the loin.

¼ cup plus 3 tablespoons extra-virgin olive oil
¼ cup honey
¼ cup cider vinegar
2 teaspoons crushed red-pepper flakes
8 shallots: 1 thinly sliced, 6 whole, 1 minced
1 cinnamon stick
1 three-pound boneless loin of pork
8 ounces dried figs, tough stems removed
8 ounces pitted prunes
3 tablespoons Armagnac, cognac, or water
4 garlic cloves, minced
2 tablespoons finely chopped fresh
   rosemary, plus sprigs for garnish
2 tablespoons fresh thyme,
   plus sprigs for garnish
   Coarse salt and freshly ground black pepper
2 tablespoons balsamic vinegar
   Grated zest and juice of 1 orange, plus
   more zest for garnish
2 cups red wine or water

1. In a medium bowl, combine ¼ cup olive oil, honey, vinegar, red-pepper flakes, sliced shallot, and cinnamon stick. Place the pork loin in a shallow glass baking dish or a large resealable plastic bag. Pour the marinade over, cover or seal, and marinate overnight in the refrigerator.

2. Place the figs, prunes, and Armagnac in the bowl of a food processor. Pulse until combined, but still chunky and with lots of texture. Transfer to a bowl, and add the garlic, rosemary, thyme, salt and black pepper to taste, balsamic vinegar, orange zest, and juice. Stir until well combined; set stuffing aside.

3. Remove the pork from the marinade, and blot dry. Butterfly the loin lengthwise: Use a large knife to cut halfway into the loin down its entire length. With the knife inside the cut loin, turn the knife perpendicular to the first cut and slice into the loin on both sides of the original cut at a 90-degree angle so that the loin will open up like a book.

4. Press open the loin with the palm of your hand. Cover with plastic wrap. Pound lightly with the flat side of a meat tenderizer or a heavy pan to achieve an even thickness, ¾ to 1 inch. Season both sides with salt and pepper.

5. Spread about half the stuffing over the center of the loin, leaving a 1-inch border all around. Reserve the remaining stuffing for serving. (The remaining stuffing will keep in an airtight container in the refrigerator for up to 24 hours.)

6. Roll up the loin starting on a long side; tie at 1-inch intervals with kitchen twine. (The loin may be prepared up to this point up to 24 hours in advance, and kept, refrigerated, wrapped in plastic wrap.)

7. Preheat the oven to 350°F. Heat the remaining 3 tablespoons olive oil in a large ovenproof skillet over medium heat. Sear the loin briefly until it is browned on all sides, about 5 minutes. Add the 6 whole shallots to the pan, and transfer to the oven.

8. Roast until the loin registers 145°F on an instant-read thermometer, 50 minutes to 1 hour, basting occasionally with any pan drippings. Remove, and transfer the loin and shallots to a cutting board or a serving platter to rest for at least 10 minutes before serving.

9. Add the reserved stuffing to the skillet and stir over medium heat until hot. Transfer to a small platter; set aside.

10. Meanwhile, make the gravy: Return the skillet to medium heat; add the minced shallot, and cook until translucent, about 3 minutes. Add the wine or water to the pan, and cook over high heat, stirring with a wooden spoon to loosen any browned bits from the bottom of the pan. Continue to cook until the liquid has reduced by half, about 5 minutes.

11. Strain the gravy into a gravy boat, and serve with the loin. Garnish the platter with rosemary, thyme, and the cooked shallots. Remove the twine from loin, top with warm stuffing, and garnish with the orange zest. Serve.

CITRUS SALAD WITH LEMON-CREAM VINAIGRETTE

SERVES 6

Use the freshest, most beautiful citrus you can find for this salad; it is delicious with any or all of the citrus listed.

½ cup hazelnuts
1 large ruby-red grapefruit
1 orange
1 blood orange
1 small head frisée, trimmed, torn into bite-size pieces
   Lemon-Cream Vinaigrette (recipe follows)

1. Preheat the oven to 350°F. Place the hazelnuts in a single layer on a rimmed baking sheet; toast until the skins begin to split, about 10 minutes. Rub the warm nuts vigorously with a clean kitchen towel to remove the skins. Return to the baking sheet; toast until fragrant and golden brown, about 1 minute more.

2. Slice off the stem and flower end of the citrus fruits. Place the fruit on a work surface, cut side down; using a sharp knife, cut away the peel and white pith, in a single curved motion, from end to end. Slice the peeled fruit crosswise into ¼-inch-thick slices; remove any seeds, and set aside.

3. Arrange the frisée on a platter. Arrange the citrus rounds over the lettuce. Drizzle with the vinaigrette, and sprinkle with the chopped hazelnuts. Serve immediately.

LEMON-CREAM VINAIGRETTE

MAKES ABOUT 1 CUP

This tart vinaigrette works especially well with citrus. Any extra vinaigrette will keep in an airtight container in the refrigerator for up to three days.

1 lemon
2 teaspoons Dijon mustard
1 tablespoon plus 1 teaspoon honey
¼ cup white-wine vinegar
½ cup extra-virgin olive oil
¼ cup heavy cream
   Coarse salt and freshly ground pepper

1. Zest the lemon, and set aside. Place the lemon on a work surface, and use a sharp knife to cut away the peel and pith in a single curved motion, from end to end. Working over a bowl to catch the juices, use a paring knife to slice carefully between the sections and membranes of the lemon; remove the segments whole. Roughly chop the flesh, and set aside. Squeeze the membrane to release any remaining juice into the bowl. Add the flesh to the bowl of juice; set aside.

2. In a medium bowl, whisk together the mustard, honey, and vinegar. Slowly drizzle the olive oil into the bowl, whisking constantly, until the mixture is well combined and emulsified. Whisk in the reserved lemon flesh, juice, and heavy cream. Continue to whisk until slightly thickened, about 1 minute more. Season with salt and pepper. Finely chop the lemon zest, and whisk into the vinaigrette.

BRAISED ENDIVE WITH ORANGE

SERVES 6

Endive is often served in salads; here, cooked, it is a side dish.

1 orange
2 cups Homemade Chicken Stock (page 119) or low-sodium canned chicken broth
1 teaspoon coarse salt
⅛ teaspoon freshly ground pepper
3 whole star anise
6 heads Belgian endive (about 2 pounds), cut in half lengthwise

1. Slice off the stem and flower end of the orange. Place the fruit on a work surface, cut side down; using a sharp knife, cut away the peel and white pith, in a single curved motion, from end to end. Slice between the sections and membranes; cut large pieces crosswise into thirds. Set aside.

2. Combine the stock, salt, pepper, and star anise in a large, shallow, nonreactive saucepan. Cover, bring to a boil, and add the endive halves. Reduce the heat to medium low. Cover the endive with cheesecloth or a round of parchment paper to keep it moist, and cover the pan; simmer until tender when pierced with the tip of a knife, about 10 minutes per side.

3. Transfer the endive with a slotted spoon to a plate, and cover with cheesecloth to keep moist. Raise the heat to high, and cook until the remaining liquid is reduced by half, about 5 minutes. Pour the hot liquid over the endive. Sprinkle on the orange pieces, and serve.

WINTER CITRUS SMOOTHIE

SERVES 4

2½ cups pineapple juice
2½ cups freshly squeezed orange juice, plus orange sections for garnish (optional)
¾ cup plain yogurt
1 banana, peeled and halved
3 tablespoons honey
¼ teaspoon ground cinnamon, plus more for garnish

1. Fill one ice-cube tray with pineapple juice and another tray with orange juice. Transfer the trays to the freezer until frozen, several hours or overnight.

2. Place the yogurt, banana, honey, and cinnamon in the jar of a blender, and blend until smooth. Transfer to a bowl, and set aside.

3. Rinse the blender, and fill with pineapple ice cubes and the remaining pineapple juice. Blend until smooth.

4. Divide the pineapple slush among four glasses; top with the reserved yogurt mixture, and place in the freezer. Meanwhile, blend the orange-juice cubes with the remaining orange juice.

5. Remove the filled glasses from the freezer, and top with the orange-juice slush. Garnish each glass with additional cinnamon and an orange section, if desired. Serve immediately.

CITRUS CAKE

MAKES ONE 9-INCH CAKE; SERVES 8 TO 10

You may choose to cut the cake and then garnish each slice with the candied peel, or to use a sharp serrated knife, and make short, quick sawing motions to cut the peel when slicing the cake.

8 tablespoons unsalted butter (1 stick), room temperature, plus more for pan
1½ cups cake flour (not self-rising), plus more for pan
¾ teaspoon baking powder
¼ teaspoon baking soda
¾ teaspoon table salt
1 cup granulated sugar
2 large eggs
Grated zest of 2 lemons
½ cup buttermilk
1 cup confectioners' sugar
2½ tablespoons freshly squeezed lemon juice
1½ cups orange Candied Citrus Peel, cut into ¼-inch strips (recipe follows)

1. Preheat the oven to 350°F. Brush a 9-inch-round cake pan with butter, and line the bottom with parchment paper. Brush the parchment with butter, and dust inside of pan with flour, tapping pan to remove excess; set aside. Sift together the flour, baking powder, baking soda, and salt; set aside.

2. In the bowl of an electric mixer fitted with the paddle attachment, beat the butter until light and fluffy. Gradually add the granulated sugar; beat 1 to 2 minutes. Add the eggs, one at a time, mixing well after each addition. Add the lemon zest; beat to combine.

3. Beginning and ending with the dry ingredients, alternately add the reserved dry ingredients and the buttermilk to the butter mixture, beating to combine after each addition.

4. Spread the batter evenly in the prepared cake pan. Bake until golden brown, about 30 minutes; a cake tester should come out clean. Transfer to a wire rack. When completely cool, remove cake from cake pan, and place on serving dish.

5. Whisk together confectioners' sugar and lemon juice until smooth and opaque. Spread over top of cake with offset spatula, allowing the glaze to drip over the side of the cake. Garnish with candied orange peel. Serve.

CANDIED CITRUS PEEL

MAKES 1½ CUPS

You can use one basic technique to make candied orange or lemon peel. The technique for candied grapefruit peel is slightly different because more pith—the bitter white layer between the outer peel and the flesh of the citrus fruit—must be removed. See note for variations.

8 oranges, or 10 lemons, or 6 grapefruits
3 quarts plus 3 cups water
6 cups sugar, plus more for rolling

1. Cut the ends off of each piece of fruit, and cut the fruit in half lengthwise. Insert the tip of a knife carefully between the fruit and white pith of the peel, and run about halfway down fruit. Turn the fruit on other end, and repeat, following the shape of the fruit and keeping peel in one piece.

2. Using your fingers, gently pull the fruit away. Reserve the fruit for another use.

3. Place the citrus peel in a 6-quart pot, and fill with enough cold water to cover, about 3 quarts. Place over medium heat; bring to a boil. Reduce heat; simmer for 20 minutes. Drain citrus peel, and soak in cold water until cool enough to handle, about 5 minutes.

4. Using a melon baller, scrape the soft white pith from the peel, being careful not to tear or cut into the skin. If you're making candied grapefruit peel, after scraping pith from the peel, simmer peel for 20 minutes more, and repeat technique to remove the remaining pith.

5. Slice each piece of peel into thin strips lengthwise, about ¼ inch wide if garnishing a cake, or ⅜ inch wide if rolling in sugar.

6. Place 6 cups sugar in a saucepan with 3 cups water; stir to combine. Place the pan over medium heat, stirring occasionally until all the sugar has dissolved, and the syrup comes to a boil, about 8 minutes. Add the strips to the boiling syrup; reduce heat to medium low. Using a pastry brush dipped in cold water, wipe down any sugar crystals that form on the sides of the pan. Simmer the strips until they become translucent and the sugar syrup thickens, about 40 minutes. Allow the strips to cool in the syrup for at least 3 hours or overnight.

7. Once cool, the strips can be stored in the syrup in an airtight container, refrigerated, for up to 3 weeks. Alternatively, to make sugared candied peel, when the strips and syrup are cool, remove the strips with a slotted spoon. Wipe off the excess syrup using your fingers. Roll the strips in sugar. Dry on racks.

NOTE: There are two variations to this method. In the first, use a vegetable peeler to remove only the outer skin from the fruit, and skip steps one through five. Slice peels to desired width, simmer in sugar syrup as in step six, then follow step seven. This technique produces thin, translucent peels that are good as garnishes for ice cream and cakes. The second variation results in wider, more opaque peels: After the outer skin has been removed from the fruit (step two), slice the skin into strips of the desired thickness. Place the strips in a pan of boiling water for 1 minute, drain, and place in the sugar syrup as in step six; follow step seven.

LIME-CORNMEAL GLAZED COOKIES

MAKES ABOUT 5 DOZEN

This unusual and not-too-sweet cookie is a nice alternative for the holiday season. For a different flavor, lemons may be substituted for the limes.

1 cup (2 sticks) unsalted butter, room temperature
1 cup sugar
1 large egg
1 tablespoon plus 1 teaspoon grated lime zest (about 6 limes)
2 teaspoons grated orange zest
2 tablespoons freshly squeezed lime juice
½ teaspoon pure almond extract
1½ cups all-purpose flour
1 cup yellow cornmeal, plus more for glass Lime Glaze (recipe follows)
Sugared Lime Zest (recipe follows), optional

1. In the bowl of an electric mixer fitted with the paddle attachment, cream together the butter and sugar on medium speed, until light and fluffy, about 4 minutes. Add the egg, and continue to beat, just until blended. Add the lime and orange zests, lime juice, and almond extract. Beat to combine.

2. On low speed, add the flour and cornmeal. Beat until well blended. Transfer the dough to a piece of plastic wrap, pat into a disk, and refrigerate until firm, about 1 hour.

3. Preheat oven to 350°F. Line two baking sheets with parchment paper. Use a 1¼-inch ice-cream scoop to form the chilled dough into uniform balls, each about 1¼ inches in diameter. (Alternatively, rounded heaps may be dropped from a tablespoon.) Place on prepared sheets about 3 inches apart. Dip the bottom of a glass in flour-cornmeal mixture, and flatten each cookie until it is ¼ inch thick (you may also use your hand).

4. Bake until the cookies are crisp and a light-golden color around the edges, about 15 minutes. Transfer to a wire rack to cool completely.

5. Transfer the rack with the cookies onto a sheet of waxed paper. Use a fork to drizzle the glaze over each cookie. Excess will drip off the edges and onto the paper below. Let glaze dry. Store cookies in an airtight container at room temperature for up to 1 week. Garnish with the sugared lime zest, if using, before serving.

LIME GLAZE

MAKES ENOUGH FOR 5 DOZEN COOKIES

The same recipe may be used to make a lemon glaze; substitute lemon juice for the lime juice in the recipe below.

1½ cups confectioners' sugar, sifted
¼ cup freshly squeezed lime juice

In a medium bowl, combine the sifted confectioners' sugar and the lime juice with a whisk until very smooth. Continue to whisk vigorously until the glaze is thick and shiny, about 3 minutes. The glaze may be kept in an airtight container at room temperature 2 to 3 hours; whisk again before drizzling.

SUGARED LIME ZEST

MAKES ENOUGH FOR 5 DOZEN COOKIES

Reserve the lime sugar syrup that results from the poaching to use in dessert glazes, limeade, and cocktails. Granulated sugar may be used instead of superfine.

1 cup granulated sugar
1 cup water
2 limes
½ cup superfine sugar

1. Combine the granulated sugar and water in a small saucepan over medium-high heat. Bring to a boil, and cook, stirring occasionally to dissolve the sugar, until no sugar crystals remain, about 3 minutes. Set aside.

2. Use a citrus zester to remove long pieces of lime zest from each lime. Add the lime zest to the sugar syrup, and simmer over very low heat until the zest is slightly transparent and very soft, about 30 minutes.

3. Place the superfine sugar in a small bowl. Remove the zest with a slotted spoon, and transfer individual pieces to the bowl with the sugar. Coat well, and transfer, using your fingers or tweezers, to a piece of waxed paper to dry. Continue until all the zest is sugared. The zest may be kept in an airtight container at room temperature for up to 4 days.

LEMON CHIFFON CAKE
WITH CITRUS COMPOTE

MAKES ONE 9-INCH CAKE; SERVES 8 TO 10

A tube pan is also known as an angel-food-cake pan. We prefer the pans with a removeable bottom.

1½ cups cake flour (not self-rising)
½ teaspoon baking soda
½ teaspoon table salt
1½ cups plus 2 tablespoons granulated sugar
6 large eggs, separated
½ cup vegetable oil
⅔ cup water
2 tablespoons freshly squeezed lemon juice plus ¼ cup grated lemon zest (about 4 lemons)
1 teaspoon pure vanilla extract
½ teaspoon cream of tartar
    Citrus Compote (recipe follows)
    Blood Orange Chips (recipe follows), optional
    Confectioners' sugar, for dusting

1. Preheat the oven to 325°F with a rack in the center, and have ready an ungreased 9-inch tube pan. In a medium bowl, sift together flour, baking soda, salt, and 1½ cups granulated sugar; set aside.

2. In a large bowl, whisk together the egg yolks, vegetable oil, water, lemon juice, lemon zest, and vanilla. Add the reserved dry ingredients, and beat until smooth. Set aside.

3. In the bowl of an electric mixer fitted with the whisk attachment, beat the egg whites on medium speed until foamy. Add the cream of tartar; beat on high speed until soft peaks form, about 1 minute. Gradually add the remaining 2 tablespoons granulated sugar; beat on high speed until stiff peaks form, about 3 minutes.

4. Gradually fold the egg-white mixture into the egg-yolk mixture; start by folding in one-third, then fold in the remaining two-thirds. Pour the batter into the pan. Using an offset spatula, smooth the top. Bake until a cake tester inserted in the middle comes out clean and the cake is just golden, about 50 minutes.

5. Remove the cake from the oven; invert the pan over a glass bottle for 2 hours to cool. Turn the cake right side up. Carefully run a table knife all the way down between the cake and the pan; invert again, and remove the cake. Fill the center hole of the cake with the citrus compote. Continue to arrange drained citrus sections on top of the cake in a decorative pattern. Top with blood-orange chips, if using. Dust the cake with confectioners' sugar just before serving. Serve with the remaining citrus compote.

CITRUS COMPOTE

SERVES 8 TO 10

Serve with Lemon-Chiffon Cake.

3 blood oranges
3 oranges
3 ruby-red or pink grapefruit
2 cups sugar

1. Slice off the stem and flower end of the oranges and grapefruit. Place the fruit on a work surface, cut side down; using a sharp knife, cut away the peel and white pith, in a single curved motion, from end to end. Working over a bowl to catch the juices, use a paring knife to slice carefully between the sections and membranes of each orange and grapefruit; remove the segments whole. Squeeze the membrane to release any remaining juice before discarding. Measure out 1 cup of the juice from the bowl; set aside. Place each segment in the bowl. Transfer the bowl containing the segments and remaining juice to the refrigerator to chill.

2. Combine the sugar and reserved 1 cup citrus juice in a small saucepan. Bring to a boil over medium heat. Reduce to a simmer, and cook until the liquid has reduced by half, about 10 minutes. Cool completely to room temperature.

3. Drain the orange and grapefruit segments, and combine them with the syrup in a serving bowl. Serve cold or at room temperature.

BLOOD-ORANGE CHIPS

MAKES ABOUT 1 DOZEN

These beautiful dried blood-orange slices are just the thing to garnish holiday desserts one edge before or after baking, and slide onto the rim of a glass.

1 blood orange
    Confectioners' sugar

1. Preheat the oven to 225°F. Cut the blood orange into very thin slices. Line a baking sheet with parchment paper, and arrange the slices on top of the paper. Place the confectioners' sugar in a sieve, and generously dust the slices. Flip the slices over, and dust the other sides.

2. Bake the slices until they begin to dry out, about 30 minutes, and turn each over. Continue to bake until the slices are dry but still colorful and not too brown, about 3 minutes more. The chips may be stored in an airtight container at room temperature for up to 1 month.

TEMPLATES

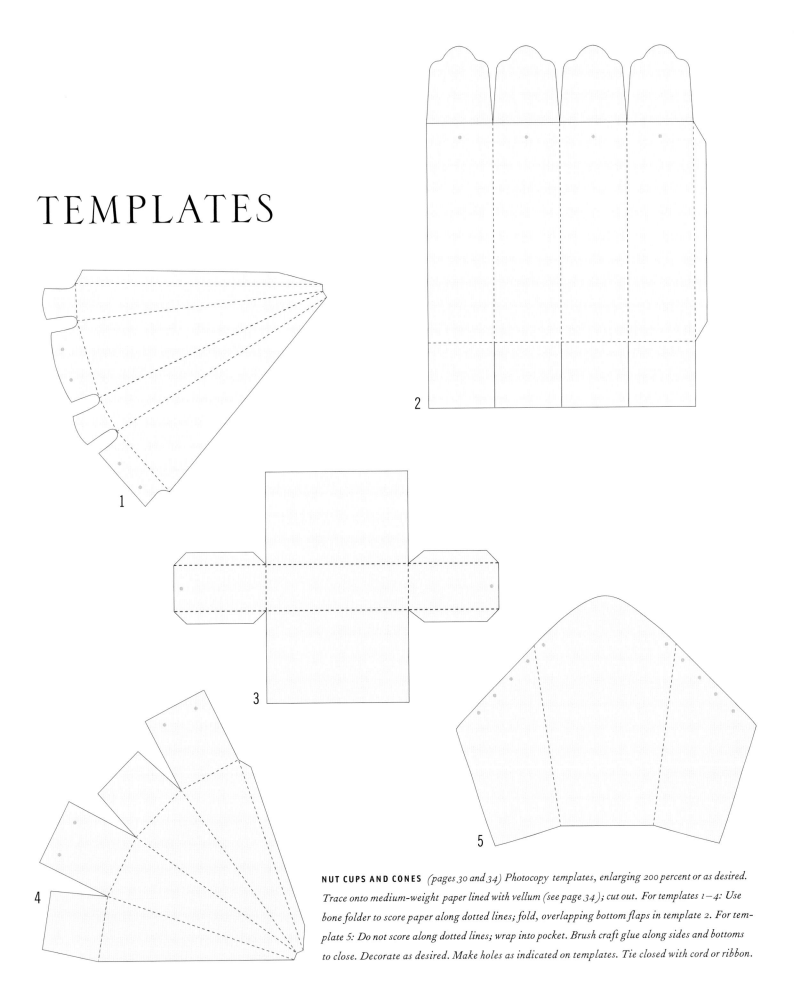

1

2

3

4

5

NUT CUPS AND CONES *(pages 30 and 34) Photocopy templates, enlarging 200 percent or as desired. Trace onto medium-weight paper lined with vellum (see page 34); cut out. For templates 1–4: Use bone folder to score paper along dotted lines; fold, overlapping bottom flaps in template 2. For template 5: Do not score along dotted lines; wrap into pocket. Brush craft glue along sides and bottoms to close. Decorate as desired. Make holes as indicated on templates. Tie closed with cord or ribbon.*

COOKIE BOXES *(page 42) Photocopy template, enlarging 200 percent. Cut out, then trace shape onto decorative vellum, art paper, or card stock. Cut out shape. Use a bone folder to score paper along dotted lines, then fold along lines, overlapping bottom flaps; secure with double-sided tape. Tie boxes closed with waxed twine.*

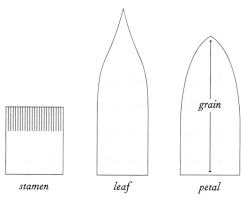

stamen   *leaf*   *petal*

grain

CREPE-PAPER ORANGE BLOSSOMS AND BUTTERFLIES

For orange blossoms at left (page 72), the grain of the crepe paper should run vertically on templates. For the butterflies below (page 75), the grain should run horizontally on templates.

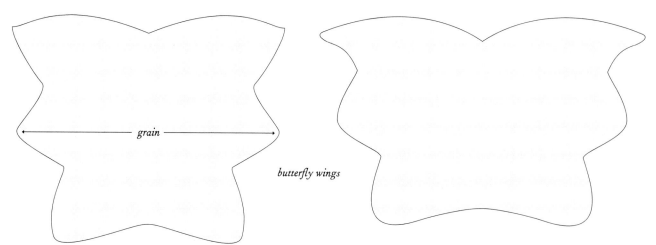

grain

butterfly wings

birch

maple

oak

VELVET LEAVES AND BIRDS
(pages 82–83 and 89) Photocopy templates, enlarging or reducing to desired sizes. Take them to an office-supply store to have rubber stamps made.

grape

fig

holly

sassafras

mistletoe

poplar

ginkgo

dove

robin

chickadee

nuthatch

135

VELVET LEAF PILLOW *(pages 84–85) Photocopy template, enlarging to fit your pillow. To do the chain-stitched stems: Insert threaded needle from wrong to right side, coming out at 1. Make a loop, and insert next to 1. Come out again at 2, holding thread loop under needle as you pull tight. Point 2 is now point 1 of the next stitch. To end a row, stitch over last loop to secure.*

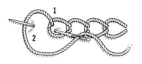

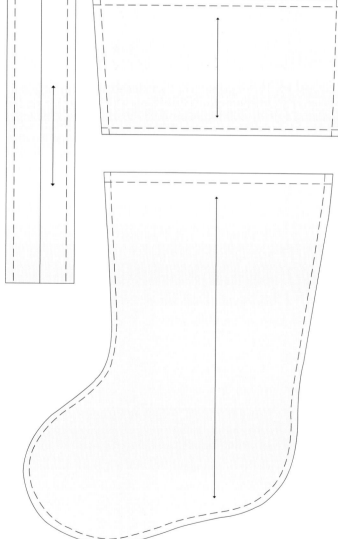

VELVET LEAF STOCKING *(pages 80–81) Photocopy the stocking templates, enlarging 400 percent; cut out. Fold fabric in half. Pin templates to fabric: Cut out two body and cuff pieces and one hanging loop. Pin the body pieces together, right sides facing, and sew along the perimeter, one-half inch in from the edge. Leave the top open. Carefully notch along the curves to allow the fabric to bend. Pin the two cuff halves together, right sides facing, and sew along the short edges. Fold the hanging loop in half lengthwise, right sides together, and sew along the long side. Turn the body right side out. Attach the cuff: Match the bottom edge of cuff with the top edge of the stocking. Tuck the cuff inside the stocking, wrong sides facing, with edges flush and side seams facing inward. Sew along the top edge; turn the cuff upward. Iron the seam open. Roll the cuff down so that it covers the seam between the cuff and the body. Fold the loose edge of the cuff under, and hem. Turn the hanging loop right side out, and sew it to the inside of the stocking at desired length.*

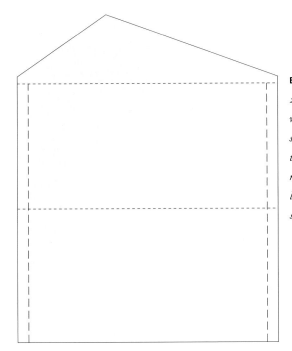

EYEGLASS CASE AND BOOKMARK *(page 86) For eyeglass case: Photocopy template at left, enlarging 200 percent. Trace shape onto leather or fabric; cut out. If using leather, score along dotted lines with a bone folder. Fold main panel along horizontal center line, wrong sides facing; topstitch short edges, leaving a one-quarter-inch seam allowance. Trim edges to one-eighth inch. Sew the two parts of a metal snap onto the top flap of the case and the outside panel; match them up so they meet when the case closes. Sew on velvet leaves and beads. For bookmark: Glue a velvet leaf to a length of ribbon with "Yes" glue. Cut out a square of velvet or other fabric to cover the leaf; glue square to the back of the leaf with more "Yes" glue. Trim around leaf.*

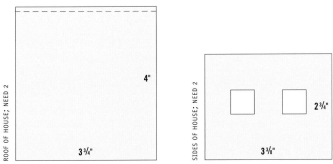

ROOF OF HOUSE; NEED 2 — 4" — 3³⁄₄"

SIDES OF HOUSE; NEED 2 — 2³⁄₄" — 3³⁄₈"

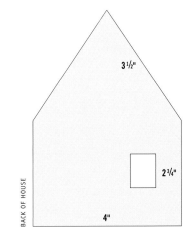

FRONT OF HOUSE — 3¹⁄₂" — 2³⁄₄" — 4"

BACK OF HOUSE — 3¹⁄₂" — 2³⁄₄" — 4"

PINECONE VILLAGE *(pages 109–11) The measurements listed are the dimensions after you've enlarged the templates. Dotted lines indicate cut lines and appear only on templates requiring two pieces to be cut out: Cut one of the pieces along the dotted lines, and leave the other piece intact. For the roof, the longer piece forms the roof's peak; the other fits snugly underneath it.*

ROOF OF CHURCH; NEED 2 — 3¹⁄₄" — 5³⁄₄"

SIDES OF CHURCH; NEED 2 — 4" — 5¹⁄₂"

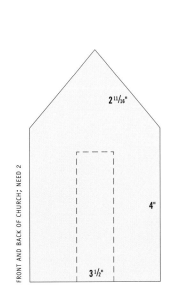

FRONT AND BACK OF CHURCH; NEED 2 — 2¹¹⁄₁₆" — 4" — 3¹⁄₂"

SIDES OF STEEPLE ROOF; NEED 2 — 3" — 1"

SIDES OF STEEPLE; NEED 2 — 6" — 1"

FRONT AND BACK OF STEEPLE ROOF; NEED 2 — 3¹⁄₈" — 1¹⁄₂"

FRONT OF STEEPLE — 6" — 1¹⁄₂"

BACK OF STEEPLE — 1¹⁄₂" — 6"

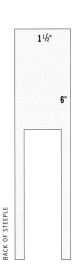

THE GUIDE

COVER

VELVET BIRD KIT (CVW005), and BIRD PRESSES SET (CVW006), *from Martha by Mail; 800-950-7130 or www.marthastewart.com.*

CRANBERRIES

Special thanks to John Decas of Decas Cranberry Co., Wareham, MA; 508-295-0147.

pg. 10

Oversized vintage SEQUINS, $3 to $6 per strand, *from Tinsel Trading, 47 West 38th Street, New York, NY 10018; 212-730-1030. $50 minimum order.* SEQUINS, $1 per bag, and pre-strung SEQUIN TRIM, 50¢ per yard, *from Toho Shoji, 990 Sixth Avenue, New York, NY 10018; 212-868-7466. $50 minimum shipping order.*

pg. 15

Baccarat "Michelangelo" footed BOWL and PLATE, $2,100 for 6, *from Clary & Co. Antiques, 372 Bleecker Street, New York, NY 10014; 212-229-1773.*

pg. 16

Silver lustreware TEAPOT, $325, *from Clary & Co. Antiques; see above.* 7" COMPOTE, from $400, *from Hôtel; 203-655-4252, available at Bergdorf Goodman; 212-753-7300.*

pgs. 16 to 17

Large Hartland VASE, $146, and small HURRICANE, $100, both *from Simon Pearce, 120 Wooster Street, New York, NY 10012; 800-774-5277 or www.simonpearce.com.* Victorian cranberry GLASS TAZZAS, $1,950 per pair, *from James Robinson; 480 Park Avenue, New York, NY 10022; 212-752-6166.*

ICE

pgs. 20 to 29

DRIED PEPPERBERRIES and BITTERSWEET, *from Dry Nature Designs, 129 West 28th Street, New York, NY 10001; 212-695-8911. $6 shipping.*

pg. 22

2"-by-3" large STAR MOLDS, $2.99, and 4"-by-5" large STAR MOLDS, six for $10.99, *from New York Cake & Baking Distributor; 212-675-2253 or 800-942-2539 or www.nycakesupplies.com.* Mini SAVARIN MOLD, (8364), $3.49, *from Fante's Kitchen Wares Shop, 1006 South Ninth Street, Philadelphia, PA 19147; 800-443-2683 or www.fantes.com.*

pg. 25

Ice-ball tray (#315), $2.19, *from Gourmac; 800-243-7700.* 8"-by-12"-by-2" rectangular CAKE PANS (BBAA-R-8), $13.40 each, *from Bridge Kitchenware, 214 East 52nd Street, New York, NY 10022; 212-688-4220 or 800-274-3435 outside NY or www.bridgekitchenware.com.*

pg. 26

24" GALLERY TRAY, *from Hôtel; 203-655-4252, available at Bergdorf Goodman; 212-753-7300.*

pg. 27

12" engine-turned TRAY, *from Hôtel; see above.* COCKTAIL GLASSES, $140 for seven, *from Clary & Co. Antiques; 372 Bleecker Street, New York, NY 10014; 212-229-1773.*

pg. 28

Plastic BUCKETS, *from Paragon Restaurant World, 250 Bowery, New York, NY 10012; 212-226-0954.* Votive CANDLES, *from The Candle Shop, 118 Christopher Street, New York, NY 10014; 212-989-0148 or www.candlexpress.com.*

NUTS

pgs. 30 to 43

CHESTNUTS and CHESTNUT SEEDLINGS, *from Empire Chestnut Co., 3276 Empire Road SW, Carrollton, OH 44615; 330-627-3181.* ASSORTED SHELLED NUTS, *from A.L. Bazzini, 339 Greenwich Street, New York, NY 10013; 212-334-1280.* ASSORTED NUTS *from Radcliffe Farms, 250 Airport Road, Bedminster, NJ 07921; 908-526-0505.*

pg. 34

Silver or copper ORNAMENT STRING (XSS002), $24 for 2,000 strands, *from Martha by Mail; 800-950-7130 or www.marthastewart.com.* Assorted PAPERS, *from NY Central Art Supply, 62 Third Avenue, New York, NY 10003; 212-473-7705 or 800-950-6111.* Assorted gold and silver METALLIC TRIM, *from Tinsel Trading Company, 47 West 38th Street, New York, NY 10018; 212-730-1030. $50 minimum order.* Victorian METALLIC SCRAP, $5 to $15 per sheet, *from Tinsel Trading Company; see above.* Also from *D. Blümchen & Co., 162 East Ridgewood Avenue, P.O. Box 1210, Ridgewood, NJ 07451; 201-652-5595.*

Assorted RIBBON, *from Hyman Hendler and Sons, 67 West 38th Street, New York, NY 10018; 212-840-8393 or www. hymanhendler.com. $50 minimum order.* Assorted BEADS, *from Shipwreck Beads, 2500 Mottman Road SW, Olympia, WA 98512; 800-950-4232 or www.shipwreck-beads.com. $25 minimum order.*

pg. 35

Pearlescent and iridescent MICA POWDERS in super russet, $21.50 for 4 oz.; brilliant gold, $10.50 for 4 oz.; copper, $13.50 for 4 oz. Duocrome colors in yellow/green and yellow/red, $11.95 for 2 oz.; Rolco AQUASIZE, $5.05 for 8 oz., or $12.90 for 32 oz.; Langnickel 1300 squirrel-hair BRUSH, $6.12; *all from NY Central Art Supply; see above.* MICA POWDER KIT (CGS006), *from Martha by Mail; 800-950-7130 or www.marthastewart.com.* RIBBON, *from M&J Trimming, 1008 Avenue of the Americas, New York, NY 10018; 212-391-9072 or www.mjtrim.com. Also from Mokuba New York, 55 West 39th Street, New York, NY 10018; 212-869-8900.*

pgs. 36 to 37

Velvet RIBBON, *from Mokuba New York; see above.* Gold metallic TRIM, *from Tinsel Trading Company; see above.* Single oat EARRINGS, $220, by Annette Ferdinandsen, and beaded white spiral all-around CHOKER (NK764GGW), $1,150, *from Tenthousandthings, 137 West 19th Street, New York, NY 10011; 212-352-1333.*

pgs. 38 to 39

Styrofoam BALLS and CONES, *from Michaels Stores, 800-642-4235 or www.michaels.com.* 12" straw WREATH FORM, $1.80, *from Boleks Craft Supplys, 330 North Tuscarawas Avenue, Dover, OH 44622; 800-743-2723 or www.bolekscrafts.com.* Round green GLASS BEADS, $14 for 9' chain, *from D. Blümchen & Co.; see above.* Chinese CUT-CRYSTAL BEADS in peridot, $11.50 for 4mm/400 pc., and $14.25 for 6mm/280 pc., *from Shipwreck Beads, 2500 Mottman Road SW, Olympia, WA 98512; 800-950-4232 or www.shipwreck-beads.com. $25 minimum order.* Kreinik silver METALLIC THREAD, $1.25 for 50-meter reel, *from Hedgehog Handworks, P.O. Box 45384, Westchester, CA 90045; 888-670-6040 or www.hedgehoghandworks.com.*

pg. 41

PARCHMENT, *from Kate's Paperie, 561 Broadway, New York, NY 10012; 212-941-9816 or 888-941-9169.* RIBBON, *from Hyman Hendler and Sons; see above.* MIRACLE BEADS in pale red and gold, *from Shipwreck Beads; see above.* Kreinik gold THREAD, $1.25 for 50-meter reel, *from Hedgehog Handworks; see above.*

pg. 42

Waxed Irish LINEN THREAD in walnut, $8.50 per 100-yard spool, *from the Caning Shop, 926 Gilman Street, Berkeley, CA 94710; 800-544-3373.* Assorted colorful waxed TWINE (CSC000), $10, *from Martha by Mail; see above.* Assorted VELLUM PAPERS, $1.90 to $2.25 per sheet, *from NY Central Art Supply; see above.* MIRACLE BEADS in pale red and gold, *from Shipwreck Beads; see above.*

pg. 43

18" PASTRY BAG, $3.99, and ½" round tip, $1.99, *from New York Cake & Baking Distributor; 212-675-2253 or 800-942-2539 or www.nycakesupplies.com.* Professional Silpat BAKING MATS, standard (KSP 002), $24, and commercial (KSP001), $38, *from Martha by Mail; see above.*

AMARYLLIS

Special thanks to the Netherlands Flower Bulb Information Center; www.bulb.com.

pgs. 46 to 51

AMARYLLIS BULBS, *from Van Engelen Bulbs, 23 Tulip Drive, Bantam, CT 06750; 860-567-8734. Also from Brent and Becky's Bulbs, 7463 Heath Trail, Gloucester, VA 23061; 877-661-2852. Free catalog.*

pg. 50

Cast-iron URN, $600, *from Joanna's Lifestyle, 1 Main Street, Brooklyn, NY 11201; 718-722-7656.* Handblown glass CANDLESTICKS, *from Distant Origin; 153 Mercer Street, New York, NY 10012; 212-941-0024.*

pg. 51

Handblown GLASSES, *from Distant Origin; see above.* Pewter FLATWARE, $264 for 6-piece place setting, *from Joanna's Lifestyle; see above.* Vintage PITCHER, *from Aero Ltd., 132 Spring Street, New York, NY 10012; 212-966-1500.* Reproduction Louis 15th-style CHAIRS, $1,250 to $1,500, *from Les Pierre Antiques; see above.*

CHRISTMAS CACTUS

Special thanks to Stephen Schuckman, of Van Vleck House and Gardens, 21 Van Vleck Street, Montclair, NJ 07042; 973-744-0837; B. L. Cobia, Joe Waechter, and Warren Empey of Cobia Nursery, P.O. Box 622677, Oviedo, FL 32762; 407-656-2870; Paul Dever of Molbak's Greenhouses, 13625 NE 175th Street, Woodinville, WA 98072; 425-483-5000; and Princeton Day School.

pgs. 52 to 59

CHRISTMAS CACTUS, *from Cobia Nursery; 407-656-2870, and Molbak's Nursery; 425-398-5100. Also from Fernlea Flowers; www.fernlea.com.*

pg. 52

MIRROR, *from Gray Gardens; 212-966-7116.* POTS, *from Lexington Gardens; 212-861-4390.*

pg. 56

Mirror-fronted SIDEBOARD, *from Gray Gardens; see above.* POTPOURRI JAR, *from Aero; 212-966-1500.* SCONCE (GPS004), $32, *from Martha by Mail; 800-950-7130 or www.marthastewart.com.* TERRA-COTTA POTS, *from Lexington Gardens; see above.*

pg. 59

TABLE, *from Les Pierre Antiques; see above.* Champagne GLASSES, set of 10, and glass CANDLESTICKS, *from Gardner & Barr; 212-752-0555.* MELON POTS, $30, *from Treillage; 212-535-2288.* CARPET (IR2797), $16,500, *from Beauvais Carpets; see above.*

FRUITCAKE

pgs. 60 to 65

MUSLIN, $1.62 per yd., *from Rose Brand; 800-223-1624.* Assorted WRAPPING PAPER, from $2.50 per sheet, *from Kate's Paperie, 561 Broadway, New York, NY 10012; 212-941-9816 or 888-941-9169.* RIBBON (#172, color 9), $1 per yd., *from Tinsel Trading Company, 47 West 38th Street, New York, NY 10019; 212-730-1030. $50 minimum order.* SEQUINS, $1 per bag, *from Toho Shoji, 990 Sixth Avenue, New York, NY; 212-868-7466. $50 minimum shipping order.* ONION SKIN, 60¢ per 22"-by-34" sheet, *from NY Central Art Supply, 62 Third Avenue, New York, NY 10003; 212-473-7705 or 800-950-6111.* STAMP PADS, $3.50 to $11, *from Pearl Paint; 800-221-6845.*

CITRUS

pgs. 68 to 79

Seasonal CITRUS FRUITS, available by mail order, *from Lang Sun Country Groves; 863-956-1460 or 800-535-1199. Also from Holmberg Farms; 800-282-3562. For more information, contact the Florida Gift Fruit Shippers Association; 800-741-1491.*

pgs. 72 to 73

LINOLEUM-CUTTER HANDLE, $4.05, and LINOLEUM CUTTERS, #2 V-shape gouge and #4 U-shape gouge, $1.35 each, *from NY Central Art Supply, 62 Third Avenue, New York, NY 10003; 212-473-7705 or 800-950-6111.* White (#16301), leaf green (#16322), and apple-green (#14652) CREPE PAPER, 79¢ a fold, *from J. L. Hammett Co.; 800-955-2200 or www.hammett.com.* 20-gauge green cloth—covered FLORAL WIRE, $3.99, *from New York Cake & Baking Distributor, 56 West 22nd Street, New York, NY 10010; 212-675-2253 or 800-942-2539*

or www.nycakesupplies.com. Green FLORAL TAPE, *from B&J Floral Supply, 103 West 28th Street, New York, NY 10001; 212-564-6087. Shipping not available.*

pgs. 74 to 75

CREPE PAPER, 79¢ per fold, *from J. L. Hammett Co.; see above.* Artificial LEMONS, $1.95, and artificial ORANGES, $2.95 to $3.50, *from Parny Silk Flowers, 146 West 28th Street, New York, NY 10001; 212-645-9526.* Bulk GLASS GLITTER (CGS005), $25 for one 2 lb., 3 oz. bag, and GLASS GLITTER KIT (CGS001), $32 for eight 3 oz. bags, *from Martha by Mail; 800-950-7130 or www.marthastewart.com.* ⅛" double-face SATIN RIBBON, $2.40 for 30 yds., *from Artistic Ribbon, 22 West 21st Street, New York, NY 10010; 212-255-4224.* Assorted METALLIC TRIM, *from Tinsel Trading Company, 47 West 38th Street, New York, NY 10018; 212-730-1030. $50 minimum order.* SEQUINS, 50¢ per yd. or $12 for 72 yds., *from Toho Shoji, 990 Sixth Avenue, New York, NY 10018; 212-868-7465. $50 minimum shipping order.* Small PINS, #8 lills, $11.60 per ½-lb. box, *from Steinlauf and Stoller, 239 West 39th Street, New York, NY 10018; 212-869-0321.*

pg. 76

Unbleached BEESWAX, cotton WICKING, WAX HOLDERS, and WAX COLORANTS, *from Pearl Paint; 800-451-7327.*

pg. 77

Vintage double damask yellow TABLECLOTH with six matching NAPKINS, *from Trouvaille Francaise; 212-737-6015. By appointment only.*

pg. 78

Vintage GLASSWARE, *from Bergdorf Goodman; 800-558-1855.* Antique damask TABLECLOTHS, available *from Laura Fisher Antique Quilts & Americana, 1050 Second Avenue, Gallery 84, New York, NY 10022; 212-838-2596.*

LEAVES

pgs. 80 to 89

Assorted celadon silk-rayon VELVET, from $29.95 per yd., *from New York Elegant Fabrics, 222 West 40th Street, New York, NY 10018; 212-302-4980.* Dark-salmon silk-rayon VELVET, $39.95 per yd.; olive-washed silk-rayon VELVET, $39.95 per yd.; and assorted VELVET, from $19.95 per yd., *from Rosen & Chadick Fabric, 246 West 40th Street, New York, NY 10018; 212-869-0142.* ACORNS, *available from Radcliffe Farms, 250 Airport Road, Bedminster, NJ 07921; 908-526-0505.* Assorted BEADS, *from Shipwreck Beads, 2500 Mottman Road SW, Olympia, WA 98512; 800-950-4232 or www.shipwreck-beads.com. $25 minimum order.* 20-gauge green cloth–covered FLORAL WIRE, $3.99, *from New York Cake & Baking Distributor; 212-675-2253 or 800-942-2539.* Green and brown FLORAL TAPES, *from B&J Floral Supply, 103 West 28th Street, New York, NY 10001; 212-564-6087. Shipping not available.* LEAF PRESSES SET, $25 for three large presses (CVW002), or 5 small presses (CVW003), and BIRD PRESSES SET (CVW006), *from Martha by Mail; 800-950-7130 or www.marthastewart.com.*

pg. 80

Winter-white CASHMERE, WOOL, and ANGORA FABRICS, $62 to $69.95 per yd.; celadon pure CASHMERE FABRIC, $99.95 per yd.; and white silk and rayon VELVET, $21.95 per yd., *from B&J Fabrics, 263 West 40th Street, New York, NY 10018; 212-354-8150.* Silver-plated 4mm BEADS, $1.99 for 100, *from Beadazzled, 1507 Connecticut Avenue NW, Washington, DC 20036; 202-265-2323.* 19th-century mahogany rectangular STOOL, $1,600, *from Mariette Himes Gomez, 504–506 East 74th Street, New York, NY 10021; 212-288-6856.* Red RAFFIA

BALLS with loop, $1.50 per dozen, *from Tinsel Trading Company, 47 West 38th Street, New York, NY 10017; 212-730-1030. $50 minimum order.*

pg. 84

American painted MIRROR, $395, *from ABC Carpet & Home, 888 Broadway, New York, NY 10003; 212-473-3000.*

pgs. 84 to 85

Floss, from DMC; www.dmc-usa.com for locations. Saral wax-free transfer paper, $5.25 for 5 sheets, from City Quilter; 212-807-0390. Gold CORDING, (M108A), $17.50 per yard, *from Tinsel Trading Company, 47 West 38th Street, New York, NY 10018; 212-730-1030. $50 minimum order.*

pg. 86

Hanging nest 18-karat gold EARRINGS, $825, by Annette Ferdinandsen, *from Tenthousandthings, 137 West 19th Street, New York, NY 10011; 212-352-1333.* Assorted VELVET RIBBON, *from Mokuba New York, 55 West 39th Street, New York, NY 10018; 212-869-8900.* Assorted LEATHER, *from Leather Impact, 256 West 38th Street, New York, NY 10018; 212-302-2332.*

pg. 88

12mm wooden-barrel BEADS, 6¢ each or $4.99 for 100, *from Vidler's 5 & 10; 877-843-5377 or www.vidlers5and10.com.* VELVET PAPERS, from $1.20 per sheet, *from Sei, 1717 South 450 West, Logan, UT 84321; 800-333-3279 or www.nagposh.com.* 4mm MIRACLE BEADS in pale red, $5 for 50 pc., $1.50 for 10 pc., and $15 for 208 pc., *from Shipwreck Beads; see above.*

WINTER BERRIES

pgs. 96 to 97

PEPPERBERRIES, *available from Radcliffe Farms, 250 Airport Road, Bedminster, NJ 07921; 908-526-0505, and craft stores nationwide.* WREATH FORMS and WIRE, *available from craft stores nationwide.*

pgs. 98 to 99

Z-Barten's Jimmy Jems Powderz GLITTER, $1.88 for 1 oz. or $13.52 for 4 oz., *from Pearl Paint; 800-451-7327.* Assorted PAPERS *from NY Central Art Supply, 62 Third Avenue, New York, NY 10003; 212-473-7705 or 800-950-6111.*

PINECONES

pgs. 100 to 113

PINECONES, *from Pinecones & Podz; www.pineconesandpodz.com.*

pg. 102

Z-Barten's Jimmy Jems Powderz GLITTER, $1.88 for 1 oz. or $13.52 for 4 oz., *from Pearl Paint; 800-221-6845.* Silver or copper ORNAMENT STRING (XSS002), $24 for 2,000 strands, *from Martha by Mail; 800-950-7130 or www.marthastewart.com.* Silver narrow Lametta TINSEL ROPING, $10 for 10 ft., and round green GLASS BEADS, $14 per 9' chain, *from D. Blümchen & Co., 162 East Ridgewood Avenue, P.O. Box 1210, Ridgewood, NJ 07451; 201-652-5595.* Jet Black 14/0 SEED BEADS, *from Shipwreck Beads; 2500 Mottman Road SW, Olympia, WA 98512; 800-950-4232 or www.shipwreck-beads.com. $25 minimum order.*

pgs. 105 to 106

Assorted VELVET RIBBONS, *from Mokuba New York; 55 West 39th Street, New York, NY 10018; 212-869-8900.* Assorted METALLIC RIBBONS, *from Tinsel Trading Company, 47 West 38th Street, New York, NY 10018; 212-730-1030. $50 minimum order.* Assorted BROWN RIBBONS, *from Hyman Hendler & Sons, 67 West 38th Street, New York, NY 10018; 212-840-8393 or www.hymanandhendler.com. $50 minimum order.* PINECONE PROJECTS KIT (CNC004), *from Martha by Mail; see above.*

pg. 106

CLIPPERS (CFT023), *from Martha by Mail; see above.* Z-Barten's Jimmy Jems Powderz GLITTER, *from Pearl Paint; see above.* Brown FLORAL TAPE, *from B&J Floral Supply, 103 West 28th Street, New York, NY 10001; 212-564-6087. Shipping not available.*

pg. 107

Red and green tinsel stem PIPE CLEANERS (t828), $2.60 for 100; 3mm white, brown, and black chenille stems (73003), $1.70 for 100; 2" chenille bumps (DJ8018), in white (010), $4 per hank, *from Bolek's Craft Supplys; P.O. Box 465, Dover, OH 44622; 800-743-2723.* Hard and soft PIPE CLEANERS, $1.25 per bag, *from Nat Sherman; 800-692-4427 for store locations, or www.natsherman.com.* ACORNS, *from Radcliffe Farms; 250 Airport Road, Bedminster, NJ 07921; 908-526-0505.* Jet Black 14/0 SEED BEADS, *from Shipwreck Beads; see above.*

pgs. 109 to 111

BASSWOOD, *from Pearl Paint; see above.* PLUGS, 99¢ each, and 6-watt BULBS, $1.49 for pack of 2, *from Rosetta Lighting & Supply Co., 49 West 45th Street, New York, NY 10036; 212-719-4381.*

THE RECIPES

pgs. 116 to 132

Professional Silpat BAKING MAT (KSP001), $24; DRIED BAZZINI FRUITS: sour cherries (KGF030), $18 per lb., currants (KGF028C), $6.50 per lb.; candied orange peel (KGF021), and candied lemon peel (KGF021), $12 per 7.1 oz.; HAZELNUTS (KGF023B), $10 per lb.; *from Martha by Mail; 800-950-7130 or www.marthastewart.com.* Candied GRAPEFRUIT PEEL (824), $9.88 for 1 lb., *from The Herbal Hut, Vier Clearinghouse, 2 Glenhaven Road, Glenolden, PA 19036; 610-586-0621 or www.herbalhut.com.* Rice-paper WRAPPERS, $3.99 for 10 pieces, *from New York Cake & Baking Distributor; 212-675-2253 or 800-942-2539 or www.nycakesupplies.com.* Black SESAME SEEDS (111 52-03071), $2.95 for 3 oz., *from Pacific Rim Gourmet, i-Clipse, 11251 Coloma Road, Suite A, Gold River, CA 95670; 800-618-7575 or www.pacificrim-gourmet.com.*

CONTRIBUTORS

Creative Director: Eric A. Pike
Editor: Alice Gordon
Senior Associate Art Director: Angela Gubler
Managing Editor: Shelley Berg
Text by Laura Wallis
Assistant Editor: Christine Moller
Assistant Art Director: Alanna Jacobs
Copy Editor: Molly Tully
Senior Design Production Associate: Duane Stapp
Design Production Associate: Laura Grady

Special thanks to Stephana Bottom, Shannon
Goodson, and Kelli Ronci. Stephana created
and styled the recipes, and Shannon and Kelli
developed many of the projects for this book.

And thanks to all whose insight and dedication
contributed to the creation of this volume, notably:
Brian Harter Andriola, Roger Astudillo, Sara
Backhouse, Celia Barbour, Brian Baytosh, Frances
Boswell, Douglas Brenner, Sarah Kaltman
Cantor, Dora Cardinale, Peter Colen, Amy Conway,
Barbara de Wilde, Nicolas DeSwert, Cindy
Di Prima, James Dunlinson, Stephen Earle, Jamie
Fedida, Stephanie Garcia, Melaño Gomez, Jill
Groeber, Brooke Hellewell, Jennifer Hitchcock, Eric
Hutton, Heidi Johannsen, Fritz Karch, Brennan
Travis Kearney, Jim McKeever, Hannah Milman,
Pam Morris, Laura Normandin, Ayesha Patel,
George Planding, Debra Puchalla, Margaret
Roach, Nikki Rooker, Andy Ross, Scot Schy, Kevin
Sharkey, Mark Ski, Susan Spungen, Lauren
Stanich, Susan Sugarman, Timothy Tilghman,
Gael Towey, Alison Vanek, and Lenore Welby.
Thanks also to Oxmoor House, Clarkson Potter,
Satellite Graphic Arts, and R. R. Donnelley and
Sons. And thank you to Martha for inspiring us to
find new ways to celebrate traditional holidays.

PHOTOGRAPHY

WILLIAM ABRANOWICZ: 9, 90, 92 (all but holly), 93, 95,
97, 98 (top right and left)

ANTHONY AMOS: 82 (bottom right), 88 (top right)

SANG AN: 60–65

CHRISTOPHER BAKER: cover, 2, 8, 19, 50 (right), 67, 115

CARLTON DAVIS: 45

REED DAVIS: 43

JOHN DUGDALE: 68

FORMULA z/s: 30, 34 (top right and center), 35–39, 40 (all
but top left), 41 (bottom right), 42, 72–77, 79, 83, 94 (right),
100, 102 (top three), 105, 106 (bottom right), 107, 112

DANA GALLAGHER: 50 (top left)

GENTL & HYERS: 80, 82 (all but bottom right), 84 (top
left and center), 87, 88 (top left and center), 103, 109–11

LISA HUBBARD: 34 (bottom photos), 52–59, 78 (all but
top left), 102 (center photos), 106 (left photos)

MINH + WASS: 6, 20–25, 28, 29

JOSÉ PICAYO: 50 (bottom left), 51

MARIA ROBLEDO: 41 (left)

VICTOR SCHRAGER: 7, 33, 40 (top left), 41 (top right),
92 (holly), 94 (top left), 96

EVAN SKLAR: 12, 46, 49

ANNA WILLIAMS: 4, 5, 10, 11, 13–17, 26, 27, 78 (top left),
84 (bottom photos), 85, 86, 88 (bottom photos), 89, 94
(bottom left), 98 (bottom center and right), 99, 104, 106
(top photos), 108, 113, 116

BRUCE WOLF: 70, 71

INDEX